MAN CITY 365

DANNY PUGSLEY

For Faith and Ruby. Love always.

First published 2010

The History Press
The Mill, Brimscombe Port
Stroud, Gloucestershire, GL5 2QG
www.thehistorypress.co.uk

© Danny Pugsley, 2010

The right of Danny Pugsley to be identified as the Author
of this work has been asserted in accordance with the
Copyrights, Designs and Patents Act 1988.

British Library Cataloguing in Publication Data.
A catalogue record for this book is available from the British Library.

ISBN 978 0 7524 5782 6

Typesetting and origination by The History Press
Printed in Great Britain

Introduction

It is now over two years since the takeover at Manchester City that saw Sheikh Mansour and his millions roll into town to herald a new dawn in the fortunes of the club. Suddenly, where there had been hope and blind faith, there was now a very real expectation. With the 2010/11 season now begun, another summer of spending saw the club on the cusp of putting an end to the long trophy drought that could signal a return to the golden days under Joe Mercer and Malcolm Allison.

However, as the club begins this ascent, it has inevitably attracted jealousy. One of the criticisms levelled is that Manchester City is a club without history. Nothing could be further from the truth. Every City fan knows the depth of history and tradition that the club possesses and the further you research and delve into this history, the more apparent this becomes.

There have, of course, been many highs and lows in the club's history. From the embryonic early days to landing the club's first trophy and then the move to Maine Road, the golden period of Bell, Lee and Summerbee, through to the relegations and promotions that littered the 1980s and 1990s, Manchester City have experienced it all. Every City fan no doubt possesses their own special memories of the club and I hope *Man City 365* serves to provide a reminder of these times. Equally, what has made putting this book together so enjoyable has been the discovery of new details, records and facts, of forgotten names and games, and not to mention the quirky events and occurrences that could only be associated with the Manchester City we know and love.

Numerous hours have been spent trawling through the history of the club using a number of books, newspapers, magazines, programmes, websites and library archives. *Man City 365* chronicles this history, covering the events, facts, figures and records for each and every day of the year.

I hope you enjoy reading it as much as I did writing it.

Danny Pugsley, 2010

January

1 January 1934

The club experienced its worst ever home defeat. 1934 had got off to a great start as goals from Herd and Bray put City two goals to the good, but from then on it went downhill as West Brom hit seven unanswered goals to romp home 7–2.

1 January 1986

A solitary goal from Mark Lillis was enough for a 1–0 win at Villa Park and chalked up City's 1,000th win in the top flight.

1 January 2002

After suffering a succession of injury troubles, the 3–1 New Year's Day victory over Sheffield United proved to be Alf-Inge Håland's final game.

1 January 2003

The New Year's Day game drew an estimated worldwide
TV audience of 300 million as Chinese internationals
Sun Jihai and Li Tie faced each other in City's clash with
Everton at Goodison Park. Goals from Nicolas Anelka and
Marc-Vivien Foe earned a point in a 2–2 draw.

2 January 1954

Goals from McAdams and Revie gave City a 2–1 victory
at home to Sunderland during the club's six-match
unbeaten run – a rare bright spot in a disappointing
season that saw the Blues end the campaign just 4 points
off the relegation zone.

2 January 1971

Only a last-minute goal from Colin Bell spared City's
blushes as they sneaked past non-league Wigan Athletic
1–0 in the third round of the FA Cup.

2 January 1997

New manager Frank Clark appointed Richard Money,
a coach from his time at Nottingham Forest, to his City
backroom staff as he began to reshape the club.

3 January 1892

The club's first ever league fixture as Ardwick witnessed a 7–0 victory over Bootle at Hyde Road.

3 January 1981

Malcolm Allison brought his Crystal Palace side to Maine Road in an FA Cup tie a couple of months after being sacked as City manager. Prior to the game, Allison ran over to salute the Kippax but it was not a happy return for him as four second-half goals saw City triumph 4–0 to kick-start their Wembley run that season.

3 January 1994

Leading 2–0 against Ipswich at Maine Road through goals from Michel Vonk and Kare Ingebritsen, the game was controversially abandoned shortly before half time due to a waterlogged pitch. It was a decision that caused uproar as it was not believed the playing surface had deteriorated from when the game had kicked off.

3 January 2007

With the transfer window having just opened, Stuart Pearce was realistic about his prospects in being able to bring in new faces, saying, 'There is no money sloshing around the accounts, so I don't imagine three successive league wins will have any bearing on the money I get from the chairman . . . and obviously, with the input he has had already, there will not be a great deal coming to me. But there are no tricks and no hidden money. We have said that from day one.'

4 January 1958

Joe Hayes got his name on the scoresheet but it was scant consolation as the Blues were dumped out of the FA Cup 5–1 at the hands of West Brom.

4 January 1975

City received a boost when the FA decreed that the FA Cup third round tie against Newcastle be switched from St James' Park to Maine Road as punishment for incidents of crowd trouble the previous season. However, any advantage this gave the Blues was not taken as Newcastle progressed to the fourth round with a 2–0 win.

4 January 2008

City outcast Danny Mills joined Derby County on loan. Former England international Mills, a high earner at Man City, had also been on loan at Charlton earlier in the season after being told by manager Sven-Goran Eriksson he was free to find another club.

5 January 1979

Malcolm Allison quit as Plymouth manager to rejoin City for his second spell in charge at the club. It would prove to be a disastrous period for all concerned as Allison could not recapture past glories and his tenure ended less than a year later.

5 January 1980

Paul Hendrie – who cost just £5,000 – scored the only goal of the game for Halifax with 15 minutes remaining to send a City side containing £1 million signings Steve Daley and Kevin Reeves crashing out of the FA Cup at the first stage.

5 January 1996

After bravely battling back from two serious knee injuries, Paul Lake announced his retirement from the game, saying, 'I have tried hard to get my fitness back but it wasn't to be. I am devastated. It's not quite sunk in yet that it really is all over for me as a Manchester City player. I have to be a realist now. I can't go on. I am told I will need more surgery on my knee. I am just gutted.' Lake came through the youth team ranks and made just 112 appearances for the club, scoring 8 goals, but was widely acknowledged to be one of the brightest talents to ever pull on a City shirt.

5 January 2010

The hotly anticipated Carling Cup semi-final first leg against Manchester United fell victim to the severely cold weather that swept across the country at the start of the year.

6 January 1894

The club fell to a 2–1 defeat away to Newcastle, a side which just missed out on promotion that season.

6 January 1897

The 5–0 victory over Walsall saw five different goalscorers get their names on the scoresheet.

6 January 1990

City's FA Cup third round tie against Millwall ended in a goalless draw. The Blues would eventually be defeated 3–1 in a second replay at the New Den.

6 January 1993

Former Blue Ray Ranson was brought back to the club
from Newcastle almost a decade after leaving to join
Birmingham. By this time Ranson was almost thirty-three
years old but an injury crisis saw him brought in on a
short-term deal until the end of the season.

7 January 1956

The away game at Blackpool was abandoned after 50
minutes due to thick fog at Bloomfield Road. The game
was replayed four days later and saw City fall to a
2–1 defeat.

8 January 1927

City exited the FA Cup at the first hurdle as a 4–1 defeat to
Birmingham saw the Blues knocked out in round three.

8 January 1990

Striker Wayne Clarke arrived from Leicester in exchange
for David Oldfield. Oldfield's spell at the club had been a
brief one, scoring 9 goals in only 20 starts, although he did

get on the scoresheet in famous wins over Huddersfield and Manchester United.

8 January 1994

Norwegian midfielder Kare Ingebritsen's hat-trick sealed City's path through to the fourth round of the FA Cup with a 4–1 home win over Leicester.

9 January 1954

A McAdams hat-trick helped the Blues earn a 5–2 victory over Bradford Park Avenue in the third round of the FA Cup.

9 January 1988

A feisty FA Cup third round encounter at Leeds Road saw Neil McNab sent off and six others booked in the 2–2 draw at Huddersfield Town.

9 January 1926

City drew 3–3 in front of almost 30,000 fans in the FA Cup tie away to Corinthians which was their first game en route to the final that season.

10 January 1953

Four goals from Johnny Hart saw City cruise past Swindon 7–0 in their FA Cup third round tie.

10 January 1957

City raced into a 3–0 lead in the FA Cup third round replay at home to Newcastle before allowing the Magpies to wipe out the lead and take the tie to extra time. Bobby Johnstone then put the Blues ahead once again but Len White hit two late goals to send Newcastle through 5–4.

10 January 1987

Drawn away to Manchester United at Old Trafford in the third round of the FA Cup, a goal from Imre Varadi was controversially ruled out for pushing as City fell to a 1–0 defeat.

10 January 2004

The 4–2 defeat at Portsmouth was notable for being the last league game for both David Seaman and Kevin Stuhr-Ellegaard. The David Seaman experiment never really worked as 'Father Time' had caught up with the former Arsenal and England goalkeeper and after being forced off with a shoulder injury he announced his retirement. He was replaced in the game by Danish youngster Ellegaard,

but the arrival of David James soon after blocked any
hopes he had of stepping up.

11 January 1986

David Phillips' goal was enough to win the points as the
Blues triumphed over Southampton 1–0 at Maine Road.

11 January 1995

Steve Lomas swallowed his tongue and was later carried
off with a cracked fibula, with Niall Quinn also limping off
as Wembley hopes were dashed for another season in the
4–0 defeat to Crystal Palace at Selhurst Park in the quarter-
finals of the Coca-Cola Cup.

12 January 1974

Goals from Denis Law and Rodney Marsh gave the Blues a
comfortable 2–0 victory over Leicester.

13 January 1906

City were beaten 4–1 by Sheffield Wednesday and exited the FA Cup at the first round stage.

13 January 1991

City fell to a 2–0 defeat to Everton at Goodison Park, a defeat that stung all the more as it came a couple of months after Howard Kendall had walked out on the club to rejoin Everton for a second spell in charge. The loss also marked the club's fourth defeat in five games.

13 January 2004

Kevin Keegan denied Nicolas Anelka was unhappy at the club, saying, 'Anelka is an excellent player. He is enjoying his football and scoring goals and I believe he is happy here. He has never come and knocked on my door and said he doesn't like it. All the time we have to live with his past and the things that have happened to him. Dealing with it doesn't bother me – it is part of my job.'

14 January 1981

City fell to a 1–0 defeat in the Milk Cup semi-final first leg at Maine Road against Liverpool. Although they drew 1–1 at Anfield in the second leg, the Reds won the tie 2–1 on aggregate.

14 January 1986

Manager Billy McNeill was offered the Republic of Ireland manager job, who agreed for him to take charge on a part-time basis in conjunction with his role at City. McNeill was keen to take the job but the City board vetoed the move.

14 January 1989

On a typically wet and windy afternoon in Oldham, Gary Megson's headed goal from a corner saw City grab their only ever win on an artificial pitch that a trio of sides used at various stages during the 1980s.

14 January 1997

The rearranged FA Cup tie at Brentford was once again postponed due to a frozen pitch at Griffin Park, enraging the many City fans who were already en route to the game.

15 January 1983

A double from David Cross ensured the Blues were triumphant against Norwich City. The win was a crucial one as it was only the club's third win over the past eleven games.

15 January 2005

Shaun Wright-Phillips netted for the third game in succession as City overcame Crystal Palace 3–1 at the City of Manchester Stadium.

16 January 1965

The home game against Swindon Town saw the lowest ever crowd for a league game at Maine Road as just 8,015 wwitnessed a disappointing 2–1 defeat.

16 January 1974

Due to power cuts around the country a generator had to be brought to the ground to ensure that the League Cup quarter-final against Coventry went ahead. Two goals from Francis Lee and strikes from Mike Summerbee and Colin Bell sealed a 4–2 win.

17 January 1948

A league record 83,260 were in attendance at Maine Road to watch Manchester United – who were using the ground at the time – take on Arsenal.

17 January 1981

The Blues came out on top in a five-goal thriller at home to Middlesbrough as goals from Hutchison, McDonald and Reeves earned a 3–2 victory.

17 January 2004

David James made his debut in the 1–1 draw against Blackburn. James, perhaps unfairly given the 'Calamity James' tag, cost just £1.3 million and was a commanding presence in goal for the club, but after indicating a desire to move closer to his family on the south coast, he was sold to Portsmouth in the summer of 2006.

18 January 1913

Fred Howard had a headline-grabbing debut as he hit all four goals in the victory over Liverpool. The prolific Howard would go on to score 40 goals in 79 appearances for the club.

18 January 1933

A Fred Tilson hat-trick saw City crush Gateshead 9–0 in their FA Cup third round replay after the first meeting had ended 1–1.

18 January 2006

The *Sun* reported that Robbie Fowler was set to be offered a new deal by the club, but only if he agreed to a 'take it or leave it' offer that would see his wages cut by 50 per cent.

19 January 1935

Despite taking on a Birmingham side who leaked an average of two goals per game during the season, the Blues were unable to break the deadlock and had to settle for a 0–0 draw that saw them lose ground to the leading sides in the division.

19 January 1991

Vinnie Jones – then playing for Sheffield United – was booked after just five seconds for a foul on Peter Reid. Unsurprisingly, Jones later received a second caution and was sent off as his side fell to a 2–0 defeat.

19 January 1996

Goalkeeper Tony Coton controversially joined Manchester United in a £500,000 deal. Despite dismaying some sections of the support, Coton always maintained that to some extent he was forced from the club by manager Alan

Ball who could not guarantee that he would be able to oust Eike Immel after returning from injury. Six months after joining United, Coton moved on to Sunderland to link up with former manager Peter Reid.

19 January 2009

The potential blockbuster deal with AC Milan for Kaka collapsed amid recriminations from both clubs, with the Brazilian saying, 'I believe I have made the right choice. To have gone to Manchester City could have been a great project but in the past few days I have prayed a lot to understand what the right team would be and in the end I have decided to remain here. I don't want anything else, I just want to be well and be happy in the place where people love me. From this story I have understood how people love me at Milan, the fans and my team-mates have helped me make this choice.'

20 January 1936

The birth of Joe Hayes. Not a name instantly associated as a City great but after making his debut as a teenager, Hayes went on to score a total of 152 goals in 364 games for the club before being transferred to Barnsley in 1965, and thus missing out on playing a deserved part in the club's golden period.

20 January 1973

Colin Bell's goal gave the Blues a 1–1 draw away at Leicester, their third such scoreline in successive games.

21 January 1928

The 3–0 home win over South Shields saw the Blues do the double over their opponents in the last ever game contested between the two sides.

21 January 2006

The high from the previous week's derby win could not be sustained as City fell to an insipid 2–0 defeat away to Bolton.

22 January 1949

The goalless draw against Manchester United was typical of the Blues' second half to the season as following the 3–2 win over Stoke on New Year's Day they would fail to score more than one goal in any of the final seventeen games of the campaign. Despite this barren run in front of goal, the club finished in seventh place, although unsurprisingly they did so with a negative goal difference.

22 January 1977

Brian Kidd hit four goals in City's 5–0 home win against
Leicester which, due to their involvement in the FA Cup,
was the only league game played in January.

23 January 1926

Managerless City recorded their biggest ever victory at Old
Trafford as they hammered Manchester United 6–1.

23 January 1932

The Blues swept past Brentford as a Fred Tilson hat-trick in
the 6–1 win helped avoid an FA Cup shock.

24 January 1959

After a 2–2 draw at Blundell Park, City proceeded to lose
the replay 2–1 against Grimsby and exited the FA Cup at
the first hurdle.

24 January 1970

Two goals from Brian Kidd saw City fall to a 3–0 defeat
at Old Trafford in the fourth round of the FA Cup. It was
to be the only defeat in five games to Manchester United
that season, as City progressed past their rivals in the semi-

finals of the League Cup in addition to doing the double in the league.

24 January 1981

John Bond saw his City side thrash his previous club Norwich 6–0 in round four of the FA Cup.

25 January 1988

Despite thrashing Huddersfield 10–1 earlier in the season, it took a second replay to knock the Yorkshire side out of the FA Cup. After drawing 2–2 and then 0–0, goals from Hinchcliffe, Varadi and White sent City through to round four with a 3–0 win.

25 January 2009

The Sunday newspapers widely reported that Newcastle goalkeeper Shay Given was expected to complete a move to City ahead of the closing of the transfer window.

26 January 1993

Niall Quinn's strike was enough to beat local rivals Oldham 1–0 at Boundary Park.

27 January 1912

During a 1–1 draw at home to Newcastle, City contrived to miss three penalties. Eli Fletcher missed the first two before Irvine Thornley stepped up to take the third – and saw his kick saved. Fortunately, George Wynn followed up the rebound to secure a point.

27 January 1974

A 4–1 defeat at Nottingham Forest in the fourth round of the FA Cup marked the first time that the club had played on a Sunday.

27 January 1979

City's miserable form against lower-league opposition continued as they were dumped out of the FA Cup at the hands of Shrewsbury in the fourth round.

27 January 2008

More FA Cup misery as Championship Sheffield United triumphed 2–1 at Bramall Lane, aided by an opening goal that saw a cross deflect past defender Michael Ball off a balloon thrown onto the pitch by the travelling City support, and straight into the path of Luton Shelton who put the Blades ahead. After falling 2–0 behind, Daniel

Sturridge pulled a late goal back but it wasn't enough to save the Blues' blushes.

28 January 1961

Denis Law must have thought the FA Cup tie at Luton Town was one of those special days as he hit all six to put City 6–2 to the good. However, with the rain getting progressively worse, the referee was forced to abandon the game and order a replay, scratching the goals from the record books. Law scored once again in the replayed game, but this time City crashed out as they suffered a 3–1 defeat.

28 January 2010

After falling out of favour during the 2009/10 season under both Mark Hughes and Roberto Mancini, £32.5 million man Robinho joined Brazilian side Santos on a loan deal until the end of the season.

29 January 1930

City hammered Swindon Town 10–1 in their fourth round FA Cup tie, largely thanks to five goals from Bobby Marshall.

29 January 1995

City were drawn away at Newcastle in the FA Cup fifth round, the third meeting between the sides at St James' Park in just over a month.

29 January 2007

The Blues were handed a tricky-looking away trip to Deepdale to play Preston in the fifth round of the FA Cup.

30 January 1897

A 6–0 loss at the hands of Preston marked City's worst ever FA Cup defeat.

30 January 1946

Forty-nine years to the day, City equalled their worst ever showing in the FA Cup as they crashed to an 8–2 defeat to Bradford Park Avenue.

30 January 1971

City's 2–0 defeat against Leeds would see Malcolm Allison later reported to the FA for his post-match comments.

30 January 2006

The club confirmed that they had rejected midfielder Joey Barton's request for a transfer, stating 'The manager has publicly stated his desire to keep the player at Manchester City. A second round of negotiations between the club and the player's representatives took place on Monday and Manchester City wishes to continue those talks.'

31 January 1968

A Mike Summerbee hat-trick helped City to a 7–0 FA Cup triumph over Reading.

31 January 1995

Niall Quinn, Terry Phelan and Alan Kernaghan were all named in the Republic of Ireland squad for the forthcoming friendly with England at Lansdowne Road on 15 February. Crowd violence from the visiting fans would mar the start of the game and shamefully force its abandonment.

31 January 1997

City signed Kevin Horlock from Swindon Town for a fee of £1.25 million. Horlock's career at the club spanned seven seasons as he helped the club rebound from their relegation to Division Two, making 232 appearances and scoring 42 goals, including City's comeback goal at the Wembley play-off final against Gillingham in 1999.

February

1 February 1958

A Sam McAdams hat-trick gave the Blues a 4–1 win over West Brom – revenge for a 9–2 defeat earlier in the season.

2 February 1929

Just three days earlier the club had played in a ten-goal thriller against Bury, but on this occasion played out a drab 0–0 draw away at Arsenal. It was the only goalless game the Blues participated in during the season and was the first of only two clean sheets recorded throughout the whole campaign.

3 February 1937

Two goals from Peter Doherty ensured a share of the spoils in a thrilling 4–4 draw against Chelsea at Stamford Bridge.

3 February 1983

John Benson took charge following the sacking of John Bond. Benson presided over just seventeen matches before making way for Billy McNeill, with a return of only three wins during his time in charge as the club dropped down the table and were relegated on the final day of the 1982/83 season after not being in the bottom three at any stage previously in the campaign.

3 February 1990

It was a much-changed City side that stepped out at Old Trafford for the 100th league derby. Following the 5–1 triumph at Maine Road, Mel Machin was sacked and his successor, Howard Kendall, brought in a number of new players to the club. City were trailing to a Clayton Blackmore header but Ian Brightwell hit one of the greatest derby goals – a twenty-five yard screamer that arrowed into the top corner to earn City a valuable and much-needed point.

3 February 2002

Stuart Pearce was the eighth player to see red during the 2001/02 promotion-winning season after he was dismissed by referee Paul Durkin in the 2–1 away defeat at Wimbledon.

4 February 1961

Two goals from Joe Hayes earned a 3–3 away draw to Cardiff, the fourth time the sides had met in a month after the clubs' FA Cup third round tie went to a second replay.

4 February 2004

If there was ever a game of two halves, then City's FA Cup fourth round replay at White Hart Lane was it. City were already two goals down by the time Nicolas Anelka went off injured on the half hour mark before Christian Ziege scored from a free-kick on the stroke of half time. To make matters worse, Joey Barton was then sent off after receiving a second yellow card during the interval. Sylvain Distin gave the Blues hope shortly after the restart before a deflected Paul Bosvelt goal reduced the arrears further. Incredibly, Shaun Wright-Phillips then levelled with 10 minutes remaining and with extra time looming large, Jon Macken sparked wild scenes as he hit home an injury-time winner to cap what was surely the greatest comeback in FA Cup history.

5 February 1913

The official attendance for the FA Cup second round tie at Hyde Road against Sunderland was 41,709 but unofficial reports suggest it was closer to 50,000 with thousands more locked outside. The game ended goalless and went into extra time but with more and more fans spilling onto the pitch due to the overcrowding, the referee was forced to abandon the game. As a consequence of this, the club was fined £500 and the game ordered to be replayed, which City subsequently lost 2–0.

5 February 1964

Despite Derek Kevan's goal earning a 1–0 victory against Stoke at Maine Road in the League Cup semi-final second leg, it was not enough to overturn the two-goal deficit from the Victoria Ground as City missed out on a trip to Wembley.

5 February 1966

Neil Young scored in a 1–1 draw at Ashton Gate against Bristol City which was the club's first appearance in front of the *Match of the Day* cameras.

5 February 1994

After a protracted and often bitter takeover bid, former player Francis Lee finally took control of the club. The move was welcomed by supporters who backed Lee's 'Forward with Franny' campaign to oust the incumbent Peter Swales who had grown increasingly unpopular after twenty years at the helm. Lee declared, 'This will be the happiest club in the land. The players will be the best paid and we'll drink plenty of champagne, celebrate and sing until we're hoarse.' However, the results never matched his early claims and the disastrous appointment of Alan Ball heralded a slide down the divisions and Lee stood down some four years later with the club staring down the barrel of relegation to the third tier.

5 February 2002

Although not short of goals during Kevin Keegan's first season in charge in 2001/02, the club spent £5 million on Preston striker Jon Macken, who had scored a wonder goal against City earlier in the season. Macken would never quite live up to expectations and would only score 12 goals in 59 appearances before moving on to Crystal Palace in the summer of 2005.

6 February 1958

After hanging up his gloves following a stellar career at the club, Frank Swift later became a journalist, working for the *News of the World*. Swift, then aged just forty-five, had been covering Manchester United's European Cup tie at Red Star Belgrade when he became one of the twenty-three who tragically lost their lives in the Munich Air disaster.

6 February 2005

City ground out a backs-to-the-wall 0–0 draw at Stamford Bridge against Champions-to-be Chelsea, leading José Mourinho to liken David James to the legendary Russian goalkeeper Lev Yashin.

7 February 1931

Goals from Brook, Toseland and Halliday earned City a 3–1 derby victory over Manchester United at Old Trafford.

7 February 1976

Ahead of bringing Aston Villa to Maine Road, manager Ron Saunders said of his sacking at City that, 'The episode is forgotten. There is no point in carrying a grudge around the rest of your life.' Goals from Tommy Booth and Asa Hartford made it an unhappy return as Saunders suffered a 2–1 defeat.

8 February 1964

After suffering a broken finger in a game against Bury, goalkeeper Harry Dowd was moved into an attacking role as there were no substitutes permitted in football at that time. Amazingly, Dowd popped up with a late equaliser to earn the Blues a point in a 1–1 draw.

9 February 1985

David Phillips continued his excellent goalscoring run but it wasn't enough as the Blues slipped to a 3–1 defeat to Carlisle.

9 February 2003

Just seconds after coming on as a substitute, Shaun Goater scored to bring City back on level terms in the derby at Old Trafford. Goater would later score again but saw the effort disallowed, leaving the Blues to be content with a share of the spoils.

10 February 1973

The 3–2 win against Tottenham was the only time in fifteen games that City scored more than one goal in a match. However, they would still score fifty-seven over the course of the league season.

10 February 2008

City travelled to Old Trafford for the derby that coincided
with the fiftieth anniversary of the Munich Air disaster.
With both sides wearing kits without any sponsors' logos
and the minute's silence immaculately observed, City
sprang a huge surprise as goals from Darius Vassell and
Benjani earned the Blues their first derby 'double' for over
thirty years.

11 February 1928

City signed Matt Busby from Scottish side Denny
Hibernian. Busby played with much note for the Blues,
playing 227 times for the club during an eight-year career.
The Scot would also play for Liverpool during his playing
career, with it being ironic that he would go on to achieve
such great success at Manchester United, the biggest rivals
of the clubs that he played for with such distinction.

11 February 1933

Forward Alec Herd netted the first of his 125 goals for the
club in the 2–1 win over Derby.

11 February 1986

A 4–0 defeat to Everton brought an end to a seven-game unbeaten run that saw the side only concede two goals in the process. The defeat, though, set in motion a seventeen-game winless streak over the remainder of the season with the team failing to score in over half of the games played.

11 February 1988

Manager Mel Machin was fined £5,000 by the FA for foul and abusive language directed at an official during a recent game.

11 February 1997

Jeff Whitley made his debut for Northern Ireland in their 3–0 victory over Belgium. He was one of four Blues who played in the game, the others being Tommy Wright, Steve Lomas and Kevin Horlock.

12 February 1955

Two goals from Paddy Fagan helped City to a 5–0 victory over Manchester United at Old Trafford – the third victory over United during the 1954/55 season.

12 February 1977

Joe Royle hit the winner as City defeated Arsenal 1–0 at Maine Road.

13 February 1978

Dennis Tueart was transferred to NASL glamour side New York Cosmos after becoming disenchanted with life at the club. In doing so, Tueart became the first current England international to move to the fledgling American league. Tueart, however, would transfer back to City less than two years later.

13 February 1997

After a brief spell at the club, German left-back Michael Frontzeck was released after making just twenty-five appearances for the Blues. Frontzeck, who spent a decade at Borussia Mönchengladbach as a player, was later appointed as their manager following the 2008/09 season.

13 February 1999

During a goalless draw at Bournemouth, midfielder Kevin Horlock was sent off in injury time for 'aggressive walking'. Jamie Pollock was also sent off for two bookable offences in a game that saw seven other City players booked. Post-match, manager Joe Royle would dryly observe on Horlock's sending off that, 'I must have missed the rule change.'

14 February 1997

It was announced that a rights issue raised £11.8 million, nearly £1 million more than was anticipated.

14 February 2006

Buoyed by the clamour for the FA to appoint an English manager, boss Stuart Pearce's odds as being the next man in charge of the national team continued to shorten.

15 February 1964

Derek Kevan was again on target in a seven-goal thriller at The Valley that saw Charlton edge out the Blues 4–3.

15 February 1992

Adrian Heath netted his only league goal of the season as City swept Luton aside 4–0.

16 February 1907

City drew with eventual league champions Newcastle 1–1 at Hyde Road.

16 February 1937

Jimmy Frizzell was born in Greenock, Scotland. Frizzell arrived at the club as Billy McNeill's assistant after spending time at Oldham and was thrust into the manager's chair after McNeill's shock departure to Aston Villa. Frizzell couldn't save the club from relegation and moved into the role of General Manager after Mel Machin took charge in the summer of 1987. Frizzell would later go on to fulfill a number of roles at the club until the mid-1990s.

16 February 1977

Goals from Brian Kidd and Dennis Tueart saw the Blues come away with a point in an exciting game at Newcastle.

17 February 1944

The birth of Neil Young. Young made his debut for the club in the 1961/62 season but it was in the Mercer/Allison era that he excelled and was the top-scorer in successive seasons in the late 1960s, in addition to scoring in the 1969 FA Cup final and 1970 European Cup Winners' Cup. Young moved to Preston in 1972 and later had a long-standing fall-out with the club over alleged broken promises in respect of a testimonial. However, this did not tarnish his legacy with the supporters who continue to hold him in great esteem.

17 February 1968

City played out a goalless draw at home to Leicester in front of a crowd of over 50,000 in the fourth round of the FA Cup.

17 February 1998

Frank Clark, unable to arrest the slide caused by the upheaval of numerous managerial changes in the recent past, was sacked. Clark had tried to introduce some stability to the club and threatened a late run at the play-offs after taking over part way through the previous season but could not build on that the following year. During his tenure, Clark often complained of there being a 'fifth column' at work and it was reported that Clark was informed of his dismissal by a local radio reporter as he parked his car at the training ground when preparing for a game against Ipswich Town.

✪

18 February 1893

Canadian national Walter Bowman became the first overseas player to play for the club (and in the Football League) when he made a goalscoring debut in the 3–1 win against Crewe.

18 February 1899

En route to winning the Division Two title, City hammered Darwen 10–0 at Hyde Road.

18 February 1996

City took the lead in the fourth round of the FA Cup at Old Trafford as Uwe Rösler smartly finished from Gio Kinkladze's through ball. Victory was denied, though, as Manchester United were awarded a penalty by referee Alan Wilkie after Michael Frontzeck was alleged to have pushed Eric Cantona shortly before half time. Lee Sharpe sealed the win for United with just over 10 minutes remaining.

18 February 1998

Joe Royle was appointed as manager. The former player was brought in to stop the slide that saw the club threatened with relegation from Division One. However, Royle couldn't stop the club from going down in his first season, but won back-to-back promotions to take the club to the Premier League. However, the club were relegated following a single season back in the top flight and Royle was sacked to make way for Kevin Keegan after a record of 74 wins from 170. His time at the club ended acrimoniously due to a dispute over his severance pay, which centred on whether the club were technically a Premier League side or not when he was dismissed.

19 February 1983

City fell to a 1–0 home defeat to Notts County that continued a run of poor form that proved instrumental in the club's eventual relegation on the final day of the season.

19 February 2006

A Micah Richards headed equaliser deep into injury time against Aston Villa earned the Blues a replay in their FA Cup fifth round clash. Richards also hit the headlines by swearing in his post-match interview with the BBC's Garth Crooks as the young defender's excitement got the better of him.

20 February 1915

City were knocked out of the FA Cup after falling to a 1–0 defeat to Chelsea.

20 February 1926

A bizarre game against Crystal Palace saw City triumph in the fifth round of the FA Cup. The Blues stormed to a 7–0 lead before allowing Palace to pull back four unanswered goals, but then resumed their dominance by scoring four late goals to run out 11–4 winners.

21 February 1934

Goals from Marshall and Tilson sent City through in their fifth round FA Cup replay against Sheffield Wednesday in a game that was played on a Wednesday afternoon watched by a crowd of 68,614.

21 February 2004

Two goals from Robbie Fowler won the points in a 3–1 win at Bolton. The victory was the only one in five games that month as the club remained in relegation trouble.

22 February 1958

City's 'century season' of 100 goals scored and conceded in the league saw many high-scoring encounters, but none as high as the 8–4 defeat away at Leicester. During the up and down season, the Blues leaked three or more goals on twelve separate occasions.

22 February 2003

Former Arsenal striker Nicolas Anelka scored City's goal in an otherwise miserable performance as the Blues fell 5–1 to the Gunners at Maine Road.

23 February 1935

A highest ever league crowd of 79,491 at Maine Road saw a strike from Eric Brook earn a 1–1 draw against Arsenal.

23 February 1963

Due to the harsh winter that season, the 1–1 draw away to Leyton Orient was the club's first game played in either league or cup since 15 December.

23 February 1974

Goals from Denis Law and Rodney Marsh were enough for a 2–0 win over Southampton at The Dell.

24 February 1940

While known more for his time at Manchester United, future City player Denis Law was born. Law played for two seasons in two different spells at the club, scoring 38 goals in 82 games in the process.

24 February 1969

The FA Cup fifth round tie against Blackburn was finally played after poor weather and a flu bug had delayed the game for over two weeks. Two goals apiece from Tony Coleman and Francis Lee saw City through to the next round in a 4–1 win.

25 February 1905

The 3–2 home win against Bury was the third consecutive game that the Blues had won by that particular scoreline.

25 February 1956

Deadly duo Tommy Johnstone and Joe Hayes were both on the scoresheet in the club's 3–0 win against Preston.

25 February 1970

Shaun Goater was born. The Bermuda-born striker joined City from Bristol City as the club were sliding towards the third tier of English football. Goater was unable to prevent the Blues from being relegated but hit 40 goals in 83 games which saw him top-scorer during the back-to-back promotion seasons as the club returned to the Premier League. Goater was stymied by injury, however, but bounced back during 2001/02, scoring 32 goals in all competitions under Kevin Keegan. However, the arrival of Nicolas Anelka restricted Goater's opportunities and he left the club in the summer of 2003 to join Reading. With a record of 103 goals in 212 games for the club, allied with his personable nature, Goater more than cemented his place in hearts of City fans.

26 February 1908

City fell to a 3–1 FA Cup third round replay defeat to Second Division outfit Fulham at Craven Cottage.

26 February 1944

Northern Ireland international Peter Doherty hit a hat-trick before half time in the 4–0 victory over Halifax Town.

26 February 1946

Colin Bell was born. Bell joined the club in 1966 from Bury with it being reported that Malcolm Allison had done his best to dissuade scouts at other clubs by talking down Bell's abilities. He helped the Blues clinch promotion from Division Two in his first season as the club embarked on a golden period of success, winning a league title, FA Cup, League Cup and European Cup Winners' Cup. Bell also won forty-eight England caps and featured in the 1970 World Cup finals in Mexico. Widely acknowledged as the club's greatest player of all-time, Bell was later voted into the club's Hall of Fame and had the West Stand at the City of Manchester Stadium named after him.

26 February 1972

Heading to Anfield in a rich vein of form, the Blues were confident of victory but a disappointing afternoon saw them comfortably beaten 3–0 by Liverpool.

⚽

27 February 1976

Ahead of the League Cup final, *Manchester Evening News* journalist Peter Gardner penned that his prediction was a 3–1 victory to the Blues. He was nearly right. . .

27 February 1999

Lee Crooks' goal rescued a point for the Blues on a tricky afternoon away to Chesterfield. The 1–1 draw saw the club continue their rise up the table.

28 February 1903

A Jimmy Bannister hat-trick saw City hammer Gainsborough Trinity by a convincing 9–0 margin.

28 February 1976

Dennis Tueart's spectacular overhead kick saw the Blues triumph 2–1 in the League Cup final against Newcastle. Peter Barnes had opened the scoring for City but 10 minutes before the break Alan Gowling levelled for the Magpies. The Blues would not be denied for long, however, and from Tommy Booth's header, Tueart won the day to see Tony Book become the first person to win the cup as both a player and manager.

28 February 1976

To cap a successful day following the Blues' triumph at Wembley, winger Peter Barnes was named as the PFA Young Player of the Year.

28 February 2007

The club announced that a fall in both turnover and matchday ticket sales had contributed to a loss of £7 million for the six-month period up to November 2006.

29 February 1992

Goals from prolific front pair Niall Quinn and David White sealed a 2–0 win and continued the club's excellent run of form against Aston Villa.

March

1 March 1924

By playing in City's win over Middlesbrough, Billy Meredith had featured in home games for the club at all of Manchester's stadiums at the time – Clayton, Hyde Road, Old Trafford and Maine Road.

1 March 1929

The club signed Ernie Toseland from Coventry. Northampton-born Toseland was known as a dazzling winger throughout the 1930s and played over 400 games for the club, later being voted into the club's Hall of Fame.

1 March 1969

City moved on to the semi-finals of the FA Cup following a 1–0 home win over Tottenham, thanks to Francis Lee's strike.

2 March 1955

Bobby Johnstone signed from Hibs for a fee of £22,000.
The Scot scored 51 goals in 189 games, including
becoming the first player to score in successive FA Cup
finals in 1955 and 1956.

2 March 1985

Steve Kinsey's goal was the difference against
Blackburn and settled the clash between two promotion-
chasing sides.

2 March 1988

The club featured heavily in a BBC TV report about the
growing craze of inflatables sweeping football. The Kippax
Stand, packed full of plastic bananas, was prominently
featured.

3 March 1900

A 5–2 defeat to Liverpool broke the club's sequence of five
drawn games in succession.

3 March 1928

Frank Roberts hit all four City goals in the 4–1 home victory over Blackpool.

3 March 1962

A hat-trick from Peter Dobing gave City a 6–2 win over Tottenham, the league and FA Cup double winners from the previous season.

3 March 1974

Despite a Colin Bell equaliser early in the second half, a goal 5 minutes from time from John Richards gave Wolves a 2–1 victory in the League Cup final. Overshadowed somewhat due to other more famous finals during that era, it was known for being one of City's more convincing Wembley performances, yet they came up against Wolves goalkeeper Gary Pierce who was in excellent form throughout the game to deny the Blues another cup final victory.

3 March 1990

Ten minutes into the second-half at the City Ground against Nottingham Forest, a largely unremarkable game was goalless when Forest winger Gary Crosby nipped in behind an unaware Andy Dibble and headed the ball out of his hand before slotting into the empty net, leaving a bemused Dibble to plead to the referee that the goal should not be allowed to stand. The referee waved away their protests with the goal standing and consigned City to defeat. Following the game, manager Howard Kendall raged, 'The ball did not leave his hand so the goal should not have stood.'

4 March 1882

The first home Manchester derby was played as West Gorton defeated Newton Heath by a 2–1 margin.

4 March 1969

A 2–1 defeat at Burnley was the first league fixture played for seven weeks due to the bad weather conditions at the start of the year.

4 March 1994

A £500,000 transfer fee saw Uwe Rösler sign for the club from Dynamo Dresden. Rösler became one of the club's most popular players due to his personality and wholehearted approach. A talented forward, he hit five goals at the end of the 1993/94 campaign before becoming the top-scorer in each of the next three seasons at the club, hitting an impressive 64 goals in all competitions. Rösler moved back to Germany in the summer of 1998 to join Kaiserslautern and experienced Champions League football before returning to the English game with Southampton. After hanging up his boots, Rösler bravely overcame a battle with cancer and later moved into club management in Norway.

5 March 1932

Two goals from Fred Tilson helped City on their way to an emphatic 5–1 victory over Newcastle United.

5 March 2003

David Bernstein resigned as City chairman. Bernstein had overseen a steadying of the ship following Francis Lee's tenure and subsequent relegation to the third tier. Although the club was back on a sound footing, Bernstein fell victim to a boardroom power struggle. He was a respected figure among fans and it was thought that some of the problems later faced at the club may not have occurred had he been in charge.

5 March 1930

After over a decade and 170 goals for the club, Tommy Johnson was controversially sold to Everton for £6,000, enraging fans who demonstrated at the departure of the popular striker.

6 March 1935

Future Blue Derek Kevan was born. While only having a brief career at the club, Kevan posted one of the best strike rates of any City player. He arrived in 1963 after playing only seven games for Chelsea following a transfer from West Brom, where he had spent the best part of a decade and had notched 157 goals. In his first season with the club, Kevan scored 30 in 46 games and then notched 20 in just 30 games in 1964/65 before suffering a knee injury that put him out for the season. The following summer he moved on to Crystal Palace after scoring 56 goals in just 77 appearances.

7 March 1903

The 5–0 win over Burton United was the sixth successive win for the club, a run in which they scored thirty-five goals and conceded just three.

7 March 1970

A year after winning the FA Cup, City headed back to Wembley to contest the League Cup final against West Brom. They got off to the worst possible start as Jeff Astle opened the scoring for the Baggies after only 5 minutes. Despite this setback, City were dominant and got their reward on the hour with an equaliser from Mike Doyle. Mike Summerbee was forced off through injury shortly after, but the Blues were not to be denied as Glyn Pardoe's extra-time winner saw City lift the cup.

7 March 1993

Bert Trautmann oversaw the opening of the newly rebuilt Umbro Stand (formerly the Platt Lane Stand) ahead of the FA Cup quarter-final at Maine Road against Tottenham. The positive mood continued as Mike Sheron headed City into an early lead to justify their tag as a decent outside bet for the competition. From then on, however, it was all downhill as a rampant Tottenham hit four unanswered goals, and fans, growing increasingly disenchanted at the reign of chairman Peter Swales vented their frustration, with a number invading the pitch towards the end of the game. The resulting scenes saw police horses used to control the crowd and although Terry Phelan scored a sensational solo goal once order was restored, it was to be a defeat which put the club in a negative light on the national stage.

8 March 1924

The FA Cup fourth round home tie against Cardiff was played in front of a record attendance of 76,166 at Maine Road. The game ended goalless but City would emerge victorious following the replay. However, their FA Cup hopes were later dashed by Newcastle who beat the Blues 2–0 in the next round.

8 March 1933

City beat Bolton 4–2 in a game at Burnden Park which was reportedly the inspiration for known City fan L.S. Lowry's painting 'Going to the match'.

8 March 1972

City signed Rodney Marsh from QPR for a fee of £200,000. Marsh was thought to be the final piece of the jigsaw that would see the club win the title in the 1971/72 season. However, from a position of strength the club faltered in the latter stages, winning only five of the final ten league games. A defeat in the season's penultimate game at Ipswich proved crucial as despite Marsh scoring in the 2–0 win over Derby on the final day, the Rams won the league by just a single point from Leeds, Liverpool and City who all remarkably finished on 57 points. During his four years at the club, Marsh scored 47 goals in 150 starts.

⚽

9 March 1960

The 3–2 defeat suffered away to Blackpool was not the ideal way to mark Bert Trautmann's 400th game for the club.

9 March 1999

The Blues' bid for promotion gathered momentum; helped by Shaun Goater's hat-trick, Burnley were hit for six at Turf Moor.

10 March 1934

The Blues took advantage of a porous Sheffield United defence by comfortably defeating the Yorkshire side 4–1 with a brace for Tilson and goals from Busby and Herd.

10 March 1971

City fell to a 2–0 defeat at the hands of Polish side Gornik Zabrze – who the Blues defeated in the previous season's final – in the European Cup Winners' Cup quarter-final first leg.

11 March 1941

Following the bombing of Old Trafford during the Second World War, the club offered Manchester United the use of Maine Road to stage their home games for an annual rent of £5,000, plus a share of future gate receipts.

11 March 1969

Joe Corrigan made his league debut for the club in a 2–1 defeat at Ipswich. Corrigan would overcome a shaky start to his City career, where he was not considered a long-term option, to become one of the club's most consistent and long-serving players. In total, Corrigan would play over 600 games for the club before moving to the NASL to play for the Seattle Sounders. He would later become a goalkeeping coach at a number of top-flight clubs and is a member of the club's Hall of Fame.

11 March 1980

The Blues signed twenty-two-year-old Kevin Reeves from Norwich for a fee of £1.25 million, realising a huge profit for the Canaries who had signed him for just £50,000 three years earlier.

11 March 2005

An uninspiring 1–0 home defeat to Bolton four days earlier brought Kevin Keegan's spell at the club to an end. After such a bright start to his time in charge, the latter days were frustrating for fans as it became clear that Keegan had taken the club as far as he could and that his policy of bringing in higher-cost, experienced players had not worked. Cutting a forlorn figure in the dugout during those final days, it was clear he was not the same man who had brought such enthusiasm to the club during his first two seasons.

12 March 1932

City had dominated the FA Cup semi-final clash against Arsenal, but in the final minute, after a Cliff Bastin shot was touched onto the bar, it was heartbreak for the Blues as the ball bounced down and crossed the line after hitting the upright to send the Gunners to Wembley.

12 March 1996

A hard-fought 1–1 draw in midweek at Stamford Bridge against Chelsea put the club in good heart for their crucial relegation clash against Southampton the following weekend.

13 March 1974

After being sent off by referee Clive Thomas, both Mike Doyle and Lou Macari refused to leave the pitch during the goalless derby at Maine Road.

13 March 1988

Mel Machin's young City side progressed to the FA Cup quarter-finals in 1987/88 where they faced a powerful Liverpool side at home in front of the TV cameras. The Blues started well but would ultimately be well beaten 4–0.

14 March 1928

The club signed duo Eric Brook and Fred Tilson from Barnsley for a combined fee of £6,000. In his ten years at the club Tilson would score 132 goals and win a league and FA Cup winners medal, but if not for injury it could have been many more. During the same period Brook would notch 180 goals, including 20 in the 1937 league-winning season where he was an ever-present. Injuries sustained in a car crash, though, brought a premature end to his playing days.

14 March 1932

Wilf Wild was appointed as manager. Wild's tenure of fourteen years in charge is the longest of any City manager, and he is second only to Joe Mercer in terms of success being the first man in charge to win the league title and FA Cup, overseeing a great period of development in the club's history.

14 March 2004

Goals from Wright-Phillips, Fowler, Sinclair and Macken gave the Blues a 4–1 victory over Manchester United in the first derby to be staged at the City of Manchester Stadium.

15 March 1960

Denis Law was signed for a record transfer fee of £55,000 from Huddersfield. Law would have two seasons in two spells at the club either side of a short time in Italy with Torino and a successful career at Manchester United. The Scot had an impressive goalscoring return, notching 38 goals in 82 games but his City career is most remembered for his goal in the Old Trafford derby on the final day of the 1973/74 season that saw Manchester United relegated.

15 March 1990

Twenty-three-year-old Niall Quinn was signed by
Howard Kendall from Arsenal for a fee of £800,000. The
Irishman showed promise at Arsenal but joined City as his
opportunities at Highbury were limited. He became an
instant hit with the crowd and was voted the club's player
of the year after his second season. A far better footballer
than he was generally given credit for, Quinn scored
77 goals in 244 total appearances before transferring to
Sunderland in August 1996 after the club's relegation from
the Premier League.

16 March 1916

City were knocked out of the FA Cup in the fourth round
after a 1–0 defeat to Sheffield United.

16 March 1929

The birth of Ken Barnes. A true City stalwart, Barnes joined
the club in 1950 from Stafford Rangers and spent a decade
with the Blues, making 283 appearances before joining
Wrexham as player-manager. Barnes would return to the
club in a coaching role under Joe Mercer and later, as a
member of the backroom staff, was responsible for the

development of a number of young players into the side during the 1980s. In 2005, Barnes was awarded a Lifetime Achievement Award by the club.

16 March 1996

Staring relegation in the face, City hosted equally threatened Southampton to Maine Road in a real six-pointer. With the game goalless, Gio Kinkladze picked the ball up just inside Southampton's half. He set off on a run, skipping past opposing defenders before jinking past a final challenge to calmly lift the ball over goalkeeper Dave Beasant. City would go on to win the game 2–1 and give themselves new hope in their bid to avoid the drop.

16 March 1998

It was announced that Francis Lee was to step down as Chairman of Manchester City and be replaced by Director David Bernstein, with the club stating, 'The whole unit are now looking forward to putting a season of unrest over Boardroom politics behind them, as they all concentrate on the most important eight games in the history of Manchester City FC.'

17 March 1894

A 10–2 defeat to Small Heath to this day remains the highest number of goals conceded by the club in a game.

17 March 1956

A goal from Bobby Johnstone was good enough to beat Tottenham at Villa Park in the FA Cup semi-final.

18 March 1933

Goals from McMullan, Tilson and Toseland saw City beat Derby 3–2 to progress through to the FA Cup final.

18 March 1972

Following his recent move from QPR, Rodney Marsh pulled on a City shirt for the first time in the 1–0 win against Chelsea at Stamford Bridge.

19 March 1881

The club recorded its first win as St Mark's in a 3–1 victory over Stalybridge Clarence.

19 March 1966

A 2–1 victory at the Baseball Ground over Derby County included a goal from Colin Bell who was making his City debut following his transfer from Bury.

19 March 1987

Long-time Blue Clive Wilson made a move to the capital and joined Chelsea for a fee of £250,000.

19 March 2005

City fell to a 2–1 defeat in Stuart Pearce's first game in charge as caretaker manager after Kevin Keegan had resigned nine days earlier.

20 March 1979

A 1–1 draw from the first leg never looked to be enough and City fell to a 3–1 defeat to Borussia Mönchengladbach in Germany to exit the UEFA Cup in the fourth round.

20 March 2006

After resting nine players in their game the previous Saturday against Wigan, City took on West Ham at home

on a Monday night – the first of the four FA quarter-finals
played on consecutive nights during the week. There
were high hopes of a trip Wembley but a brace from
Dean Ashton put the Hammers ahead and despite Kiki
Musampa's late goal, the Blues crashed out once again at
the quarter-final stage.

21 March 1990

A bullet header from Niall Quinn on his debut earned City
a point in their 1–1 draw at Chelsea.

21 March 1996

Facing a battle against relegation, the club made a
controversial decision to accept a £3.6 million bid from
Blackburn for midfielder Gary Flitcroft. The former youth
team player was a key member of the squad and had
made 134 appearances for the Blues when he departed for
Ewood Park.

22 March 1969

A goal from Tommy Booth helped City past Everton in the
FA Cup semi-final tie staged at Villa Park.

22 March 1980

Mickey Thomas' goal ensured a 1–0 win for Manchester United in what was the 100th Manchester derby.

22 March 1986

Just twenty-four hours before their appearance in the Full Members' Cup final, City had to contest the Manchester derby. After going 2–0 down, goals from Clive Wilson and an Arthur Albiston own goal earned City a point and put the side in good heart for the trip to Wembley.

23 March 1895

Aided by four goals from McReddie and a brace by Meredith, the club recorded their highest ever victory by thrashing Lincoln 11–3.

23 March 1986

Victories over Leeds, Sheffield United and Sunderland, before a two-legged win against Hull in the Northern final, booked a date with Chelsea in the inaugural Full Members' Cup final in front of a 68,000 crowd at Wembley. Quite remarkably, both sides had also played league fixtures the day before but this did not detract from the final – in fact the game produced a minor classic. Steve Kinsey put City ahead after 10 minutes before Chelsea steamrollered the Blues by scoring five unanswered goals, including a hat-trick from David Speedie. With despondent fans drifting out of Wembley as time ticked away, City came storming back. Scoring three goals in the final 6 minutes through Mick MCarthy, a Doug Rougvie own goal and Mark Lillis, the comeback to end all comebacks was suddenly on the cards. However, and despite mounting City pressure, Chelsea held firm though to lift the trophy.

24 March 1967

The 3–1 defeat to Blackpool was the first time in twelve matches involving City that either side had scored more than one goal.

24 March 1971

Ian Mellor scored in just his second game for the club as City beat Gornik Zabrze 2–0 to overturn a two-goal deficit from the first leg in the return game at Maine Road, forcing a replay in their European Cup Winners' Cup tie in the days before penalty shoot-outs were introduced to European football. City would go on to win 3–1 in the replay which was staged in Copenhagen.

24 March 1994

While most speculation at the time linked Anders Limpar with a move to the club, it was Everton winger Peter Beagrie who was signed for a fee of around £1 million to cap a spell of transfer activity that saw Uwe Rösler and Paul Walsh arrive earlier in the month. Just one place above the relegation zone heading into March, the attacking moves from manager Brian Horton paid dividends as form improved and the Blues hauled themselves out of danger.

25 March 1978

A double from Mick Channon was enough to earn a share of the spoils at home to Middlesbrough in a match that ended 2–2.

25 March 1989

An astonishing game at the Bescot Stadium saw City fall 2–0 down to Walsall and then have goalkeeper Andy Dibble forced off through injury. Midfielder Nigel Gleghorn donned the gloves and the Blues launched an astonishing comeback as a double from Paul Moulden helped earn a point in a thrilling 3–3 draw.

26 March 1921

The 3–0 victory over Burnley was played in front of a 47,500 crowd – the highest recorded attendance at Hyde Road. The victory also ended a stretch of thirty games without defeat for the Lancashire side.

26 March 1955

A solitary Roy Clarke goal was enough to send City through to Wembley at the expense of Sunderland in the FA Cup semi-final.

27 March 1920

The 2–1 home win over Liverpool was attended by King George V – the first time a reigning monarch had attended a provincial football match.

27 March 1926

Two goals from Tommy Browell saw City past rivals Manchester United 3–0 en route to that season's FA Cup final.

28 March 1964

Bert Trautmann made his 545th and final appearance for the club in a 2–0 defeat at Preston in Division Two, a game that was played just twenty-four hours after a 5–0 win over Norwich.

29 March 1924

City crashed out 2–0 to Newcastle in the FA Cup semi-final at St Andrews in a game that would become famous for featuring a forty-nine-year-old Billy Meredith. Meredith had returned to the club in 1921 following his time at Manchester United, but it was to be disappointing finale for one of the finest players to ever pull on a City shirt. City had played well but fell behind to two goals from Neil Harris, at which point Newcastle adopted a defensive outlook which the Blues had no answer to.

29 March 1932

The Blues' 5–1 victory over Birmingham at St Andrews was the second victory in successive days against the Midlanders after City had triumphed 2–1 at Maine Road just twenty-four hours earlier.

30 March 1929

Tommy Johnson's opener in the 4–1 victory over Burnley was his thirty-second of the season, establishing a new club record. To date, only Francis Lee in 1971/72 has reached a similar total.

30 March 1960

City's 3–1 win over West Ham featured a controversial moment. With the Hammers leading 1–0, a penalty was awarded when debutant Denis Law was fouled in the box. The penalty was taken by Ken Barnes who ran up and simply touched the ball forward for Billy McAdams to strike the ball home. The goal was initially given, but after protests from the West Ham players the referee overturned his original decision and ordered the kick to be retaken – which Barnes went on to miss.

30 March 1973

Malcolm Allison resigned as manager. Two years earlier, Allison had taken sole control of the club in a move which led to the move 'upstairs' and ultimately the departure of Joe Mercer. Allison fell just short of the title in his first season in charge, and landed the Charity Shield in his second but felt that he could not motivate himself or the side any further. After departing the club, Allison soon took up the manager's seat at Crystal Palace.

30 March 1991

After a lifeless first half, the home game against Southampton exploded into action as six second-half goals saw the two sides share a 3–3 draw, with the Saints snatching a late equaliser through Alan McLoughlin.

31 March 1973

Tony Towers' goal was good enough for a 1–0 victory over Leeds, a positive way to end what had been a miserable March for the club that saw them draw one and lose five of the previous six games during the month.

31 March 2001

A 3–1 defeat at home to Aston Villa pushed the Blues further into relegation trouble and four points from safety with just seven games remaining.

April

1 April 1950

Never a happy hunting ground for the club, a trip to Highbury saw City once again come away empty-handed thanks to a 4–1 defeat.

1 April 1972

City's bid for the league title hit the skids following a 2–1 home defeat to relegation-threatened Stoke. With just six games remaining, City, Derby, Leeds and Liverpool were all bunched closely together at the top of the table.

2 April 1923

City's 1–0 win over Sunderland was the final victory at Hyde Road. Ironically, nearly eighty years later the same opponents were also the last team to be beaten at Maine Road.

2 April 2007

New signing Emile Mpenza extolled the virtues of
Manchester in an interview with the official website,
and looked ahead to securing a more permanent deal at
the end of the season; 'I've enjoyed being at City since I
arrived and I think it's going well for me. I'm just going to
keep working hard, but I like it here and if I get some more
goals then maybe we can talk when the season is finished.
I've been to London and Birmingham in the past, but
Manchester has everything and I think it's a great vibrant
city – it suits me down to the ground.'

2 April 1994

Goals from Beagrie, Rösler and Walsh gave the Blues'
hopes of avoiding relegation a huge boost as Aston Villa
were defeated 3–0 at Maine Road. It was the first of three
victories in a week that ultimately saw the club avoid the
drop by only three points.

3 April 1896

City drew 1–1 at home to Liverpool, a result that ensured
the Blues would eventually be pipped to the Division Two
title that season on goal difference after the two sides had
finished level on points.

3 April 1965

Plymouth were defeated 2–1 at Maine Road, a game that saw a certain Malcolm Allison on the visitors' bench just a couple of months before he arrived at the club to work alongside newly appointed manager Joe Mercer.

4 April 1992

The 4–0 win over Leeds was the thirteenth clean sheet of the season recorded by Tony Coton, who had just been named in the PFA team of the season.

5 April 2000

The 2–0 victory over Bolton saw City leapfrog Barnsley into second place in the table and maintain the club's hopes of automatic promotion back to the Premier League.

6 April 1926

The club played their third game in just four days as they took on Burnley at Turf Moor. Goals from Hicks and

Johnson were enough for a 2–1 win but it was the only victory out of the three games. Despite a late rally at the end of the season, they could not avoid relegation.

6 April 2002

A Darren Huckerby hat-trick helped City to a 5–1 rout over Barnsley and to seal the Division One title under Kevin Keegan with two games remaining. The attacking style during the 2001/02 season saw the side score 108 goals and amass 99 points.

7 April 1948

The away derby against Manchester United in the 1947/48 season was actually played at Maine Road due to the damage sustained to Old Trafford during the war. A crowd of 71,690 saw the sides play out a 1–1 draw.

7 April 1992

A late Keith Curle penalty after Steve Bruce had brought down David White earned a hard-fought point in a 1–1 draw in the derby at Old Trafford.

8 April 1899

A Williams brace defeated Small Heath 2–0 and secured the Division Two title under the management of Sam Ormerod – it was the first honour in the club's history.

8 April 1912

The 2–0 win over Tottenham sparked a run of four consecutive victories to haul City away from the relegation zone to safety at the end of the season.

9 April 1922

The club officially announced the building of a new stadium close to Moss Side and Rusholme that would replace the current stadium at Hyde Road after failing to secure a move to Belle Vue. The stadium, of course, would go on to be known as Maine Road.

10 April 1937

Goals from Ernie Toseland and Peter Doherty won the points in a vital game at home to Arsenal, a match-up between the top two teams in the table. The win saw the

Blues move ahead of the Gunners with only four games remaining.

11 April 1896

City tasted defeat in the final of the Manchester Senior Cup after finishing on the wrong end of a 2–1 scoreline against Bury.

11 April 1962

At 15 years and 314 days, Glyn Pardoe became the youngest player to ever play for the club in the 4–1 defeat against Birmingham. In a playing career spanning fourteen seasons, Pardoe made 378 appearances for the club and would later be a valuable part of the backroom staff during the 1980s.

11 April 1974

After only five months at the helm, and having been lauded by new Chairman Peter Swales as the perfect choice for the club, manager Ron Saunders was shown the door – this despite his having guided City to the final of the League Cup earlier in the season. He could not match this success in the league, however, winning only six of twenty-one games amid reports of player unrest.

11 April 1981

In front of a packed City contingent in the Holte End at Villa Park, skipper Paul Power crashed home a free-kick in extra time to break the deadlock and send City to Wembley with a 1–0 win over Ipswich in the FA Cup semi-final.

11 April 2001

Goalkeeper Carlo Nash made his debut at home to Arsenal and, without making a save, saw his side 4–0 down to a rampant Gunners side after just 35 minutes. Perhaps the only positive to take from the game was that the side didn't concede again.

12 April 1894

It was announced that Ardwick would be renamed as Manchester City at the conclusion of the 1893/94 season.

12 April 1972

Francis Lee's first goal in the 3–1 derby victory over Manchester United was his thirtieth league goal of the season.

12 April 1974

Tony Book was appointed as the club's new manager. Book would spend just over five years in charge, becoming the first person to win the League Cup as both a player and manager. Book's sides were renowned for playing good football and he guided City to a number of respectable league positions, but in July 1979 he was moved upstairs as Peter Swales brought back Malcolm Allison. This led to the break-up of the side and ended the period of success over the past decade or so. Swales would later rue the decision, calling it the 'biggest mistake' that he made while in charge.

12 April 1980

Goals from Kevin Reeves and Dennis Tueart sealed a 2–1 win over Wolves and ended a seventeen-match winless streak that blighted Malcolm Allison's second spell in charge.

13 April 1894

A memorandum was signed to incorporate Manchester City FC as a limited company, with the aims of the club being to promote not only football but a wide number of different sports.

13 April 1985

A disappointing run of form continued as City were thrashed 4–1 away at Grimsby. Having led the league at the end of March, the result meant City dropped to fifth place and out of the promotion places.

14 April 1900

City suffered a 3–1 defeat against Sunderland in a game which saw keeper Charlie Williams score with a kick from his own area with the assistance of a strong wind behind him.

14 April 1973

City's attacking prowess was too much for Sheffield United as Colin Bell, Francis Lee and Rodney Marsh all scored to give the Blues a 3–1 victory.

15 April 1927

The 2–2 draw at Darlington was the first of two successive results in consecutive days in the North-East as the club also drew by the same scoreline at South Shields the following day.

15 April 1970

Heading into the game 1–0 down from the first leg, City demolished German side Schalke 04 5–1 in the return fixture. Goals from Doyle, Young and Bell and two from Neil Young saw the Blues cruise into the European Cup Winners' Cup final.

16 April 1898

Hat-tricks from both Whitehead and Meredith helped City run riot as they put nine unanswered goals past Burton Swifts.

16 April 2008

A 3–1 victory at the City of Manchester Stadium gave City's youth side a 4–2 aggregate win over Chelsea in the FA Youth Cup final.

17 April 1893

Ardwick brought a close to their first ever season in the Football League with a 3–1 victory over Lincoln.

17 April 1937

A headed goal from Peter Doherty in the 5–2 victory over Preston was the club's 100th league goal of the season.

18 April 1891

A David Weir goal was enough to give the Blues their first Manchester Senior Cup win as they defeated Newton Heath 1–0.

18 April 1972

The Blues slipped to a 2–1 defeat against rivals Ipswich Town that caused serious damage to their hopes of winning the title.

19 April 1958

Legendary figure Billy Meredith died in Withington, Manchester, aged eighty-three.

19 April 1980

Goals from Deyna, Robinson and Tueart in a 3–1 win over
Bristol City ended a nine-game winless streak at Maine
Road, easing their relegation fears in the process.

20 April 1929

Ernie Toseland made his debut for the club in the 3–1
victory over Bury.

20 April 1991

Following the sending-off of goalkeeper Tony Coton,
forward Niall Quinn took over the gloves. Having already
scored earlier in the game, Quinn endeared himself to City
fans even further as he kept out Dean Saunders' penalty to
preserve the 2–1 win and condemn Derby to relegation.

21 April 1951

An entertaining afternoon at Maine Road saw Barnsley
well beaten 6–0 with Roy Clarke scoring twice.

21 April 2002

The 3–1 victory at home to Portsmouth on the final day of the season was the thirty-first of the campaign and set a new record for league victories in a single campaign.

21 April 2003

A 3–0 win over Sunderland was the final victory seen at Maine Road before the move to the City of Manchester Stadium. The victory was largely earned thanks to a double from Marc-Vivien Foe, the second of which would prove to be the last ever City goal at the famous stadium.

22 April 2007

Amid rumours of a lower than anticipated take-up rate for season tickets, the club announced that they had decided to extend the original cut-off date for renewals.

23 April 1892

The club lifted the Manchester Cup for the second year in succession as Ardwick defeated Bolton Wanderers 4–1.

23 April 1904

In front of a crowd of 61,374 at Crystal Palace, City became the first Manchester side to win a significant trophy as they defeated Bolton 1–0 in the FA Cup final thanks to a first-half goal from captain Billy Meredith. The homecoming parade to welcome the victorious side back to Manchester had to be delayed until the Monday evening after the club had played their final league fixture at Everton.

23 April 1910

Goals from Conlin, Dorsett and Wynn in a 3–0 win over Leeds earned City promotion back to the top flight at the first attempt. Despite a last-day defeat at Wolves, City would also go on to win the title that season.

23 April 1991

David White scored four times as City romped to a 5–1 win over Aston Villa.

24 April 1926

A goal from David Jack with little under 15 minutes remaining condemned City to defeat in the FA Cup final against Bolton.

24 April 1937

With only two games remaining in the 1936/37 season,
just one victory would see City win their first ever title.
Relegation-haunted Sheffield Wednesday visited Maine
Road and were swept aside as City went three goals to
the good inside of 12 minutes with Peter Doherty scoring
twice. Although Wednesday pulled a goal back, Eric Brook
restored the lead to see the Blues run out 4–1 winners with
the final whistle sparking wild scenes as fans raced on to
the pitch to celebrate the club's first championship.

24 April 2007

Former City player Ray Ranson was the key figurehead of
a group that made an indicative proposal to the current
board to take control of the club.

24 April 2010

After replacing the injured Shay Given, Gunnar Nielsen
became the first Faroe Islander to play in the Premier
League when he made his debut in the 0–0 draw
against Arsenal.

25 April 1914

The point earned in the 2–2 draw against Preston was enough to see City finish ahead of Manchester United for the first time since the 1905/06 season.

25 April 1925

A crowd of 15,000 saw a combined Manchester XI take on a Glasgow XI in Billy Meredith's testimonial game.

26 April 1926

Following a period where the club was led by committee members, a permanent manager in the shape of Peter Hodge was finally appointed. Hodge was in charge for just under six years, helping put in place some of the foundations that led to success in the 1930s.

26 April 1958

The two goals conceded on the final day of the 1957/58 season meant that City finished the season having scored and conceded more than 100 goals. The season would later be chronicled in Dave Wallace's book *Century City*.

26 April 1969

A left-footed strike from Neil Young after 23 minutes won the FA Cup for City as they defeated Leicester 1–0. Not a classic, the game was, however, played in a fine spirit and although Leicester were at the wrong end of the table they pushed City harder than many anticipated. Young's strike, however, would ensure that he would be fondly remembered alongside the greats of that era.

26 April 2005

Despite the disappointment of missing out on the PFA Young Player of the Year award, Shaun Wright-Phillips received the accolade of being named in the Premier League team of the season.

27 April 1957

A tense final game of the season away to Birmingham saw the lead change back and forth before ending in a 3–3 draw that was enough to ensure the club was safe from relegation despite the sides below City still having games to play.

27 April 1974

Heading into the Manchester derby on the final day of the season, United were mired deep in relegation trouble and the encounter between the two sides was heading to a goalless draw when Denis Law, with his back to goal, backheeled a cross beyond Alex Stepney to put the Blues ahead. Facing dropping out of the top flight, Manchester United fans invaded the pitch and the players were taken off the field, and did not return. It was decreed that the 1–0 scoreline would stand and although results elsewhere meant United would have been relegated regardless, Law's goal would always be known as the one that sent Manchester United down.

28 April 1909

City were defeated 1–0 at Bristol City and relegated in a game where a point would have been enough to keep the club in the top flight.

28 April 1923

The final game ever played at Hyde Road saw City and Newcastle play out a goalless draw.

28 April 1934

Two goals from Fred Tilson in the last 15 minutes won the FA Cup final as City came from a goal down to defeat Portsmouth 2–1. At half time Tilson had reportedly promised Frank Swift that he would score the two goals needed after Swift had blamed himself for Portsmouth's opener.

28 April 1971

With the club struggling with injuries at the end of a hard season, City suffered a 1–0 defeat at Stamford Bridge in the semi-finals of the European Cup Winners' Cup. They crashed out 2–0 on aggregate in the defence of the trophy they had won twelve months earlier.

29 April 1905

During the 3–2 defeat at Aston Villa, Billy Meredith was alleged to have offered Alec Leake £10 to lose the crucial league game. As a result of the ensuing investigation, seventeen players and officials received suspensions of up to a year in length. Most of the players who were suspended would later sign for Manchester United and formed the basis of their first successful side.

29 April 1933

City were defeated 3–0 by Everton in the FA Cup final. The game would see City wear red shirts that were numbered 12–22, with Everton sporting the more traditional 1–11 digits.

29 April 1959

The Blues beat Leicester City 3–1 on the last day of the campaign to move out of the relegation places and instead condemn Aston Villa to relegation.

29 April 1968

City's 2–0 victory over Everton, coupled with a defeat for Manchester United, saw the Blues move to the top of the table with just two fixtures remaining.

29 April 1970

A goal from Neil Young and a Francis Lee penalty saw City defeat Polish side Gornik Zabrze 2–1 in Vienna to record the club's first and only European trophy. The Blues dominated the opening stages and Young put them ahead on 12 minutes after good work from Lee. Lee then doubled the lead just before the half-time whistle from the penalty spot. With the rain getting heavier and heavier, Gornik pulled a goal back to cause concern, but the Blues were strong enough to hold on for the victory.

29 April 1986

Goals from David Boyd and Paul Moulden sealed the 2–0 victory to win the FA Youth Cup against Manchester United.

29 April 1995

Veteran John Burridge became the oldest player to play in the Premier League when, aged 43 years and 148 days old, he kept a clean sheet in City's goalless draw against Newcastle.

30 April 1977

In a bad-tempered encounter, City were defeated 4–0 at the Baseball Ground against Derby County which all but handed Liverpool the title. The game saw a bizarre incident where Joe Corrigan challenged the spot where a penalty kick had been placed, pacing out the twelve yards himself which led to the spot being repainted.

30 April 1993

Former City player Tommy Caton died aged just thirty after suffering a heart attack. Caton, who played in the 1981 FA Cup final, made his debut in August 1979 aged sixteen and made 165 appearances before joining Arsenal.

30 April 1994

The 2–2 draw against Chelsea was the final game played in front of the terraced Kippax Street Stand. Following the game, work began on a new all-seater stand at Maine Road and an emotional day saw fans relive their memories of years gone by as they bade farewell to the famous old stand.

30 April 1996

Keith Curle was cleared of a misconduct charge stemming from an incident with Tino Asprilla in the recent game with Newcastle. Asprilla, however, was fined £10,000 and banned for one match.

May

1 May 1926

Just one week after losing in the FA Cup final, City were defeated 3–2 at Newcastle and were relegated after both Burnley and Leeds had last-day victories to leapfrog the Blues. The game would, though, see both Roberts and Browell get on the scoresheet to take their combined strike pairing tally to 58 goals for the season, a record that is still to be bettered.

1 May 1989

For the second time in the season, Nigel Gleghorn was forced to don the goalkeeping gloves after Andy Dibble suffered an injury. Gleghorn had scored the Blues' goal earlier in the game and helped his side earn a 1–1 draw at home to Crystal Palace.

1 May 2007

Joey Barton was suspended by the club following a training ground incident with Ousmane Dabo that left the

Frenchman suffering cuts and bruises. Barton would never play for the club again as during the subsequent off-season he was sold to Newcastle for £5.5 million.

2 May 1992

A David White hat-trick in the 5–2 win over Oldham ensured the Blues finished in fifth place in Division One for the second successive season.

2 May 1996

Former chairman Peter Swales' death came just days before the game that would see the club relegated. Swales had been ousted in the previous season as Francis Lee was carried to power on a wave of popular support from fans who had grown tired of failure and a procession of managers under Swales' reign. Despite his lack of popularity at the end of his time in charge, the minute's silence prior to the game against Liverpool the following weekend was immaculately observed.

3 May 1947

The 2–0 home loss to Newcastle ended a record-equalling twenty-two games without defeat.

3 May 1998

Results elsewhere meant that a 5–2 thrashing of Stoke on the final day of the season was not enough to stop City spiralling into the third tier of English football for the first time ever.

4 May 1929

Tommy Johnson's goal in the 1–1 draw against Liverpool on the final day of the season meant that the striker finished the season having scored thirty-eight league goals, a club record that still stands.

4 May 1966

Colin Bell's goal was enough to beat Rotherham and see City promoted back to Division One, heralding the start of the club's golden era under Joe Mercer and Malcolm Allison.

4 May 1984

City's 2–0 home defeat to Chelsea was the first match in the second tier of English football to be shown live. The game was broadcast on a Friday evening by the BBC.

5 May 1928

Despite a last-day defeat at Notts County, the Blues secured the Division Two title. Not only did the club go up as champions, but their average attendance of 37,468 was a league best.

5 May 1956

City lifted the FA Cup with a 3–1 victory over Birmingham that will be forever remembered for the game in which Bert Trautmann broke his neck. Goals from Hayes, Dyson and Johnstone had put the Blues on the road to victory when Trautmann was injured in a collision with a Birmingham forward. Faced with the prospect of playing with ten men, Trautmann elected to continue on, not knowing the severity of the injury he had sustained.

5 May 1971

Prior to the home derby against Manchester United on the final day of the season, former City player and then United manager Matt Busby was presented with the *This is Your Life* book by show host Eamonn Andrews, leading to a surreal atmosphere throughout the game.

5 May 1996

After winning their two previous games against Sheffield Wednesday and Aston Villa, City had the opportunity of an improbable escape in the final match of the season at home to Liverpool. The Blues fell behind to Liverpool early, but goals from Rösler and Symons levelled matters up. Believing that a point was enough and with the clock running down, City began to play out time before it was realised that a victory was needed due to results elsewhere. The Blues couldn't get the winner and were relegated on goal difference.

5 May 2010

Hopes of a first ever Champions League qualification were extinguished as Peter Crouch hit a late winner to secure fourth spot for Tottenham.

6 May 1950

Trailing Charlton by a point heading into the final game of the season, a terrible performance saw the Blues beaten 3–1 away at Everton and subsequently relegated to Division Two.

6 May 1985

City fell to a disappointing 3–2 defeat at Notts County when a win would have sealed promotion to Division One under Billy McNeill. The game was also marred throughout by trouble on the terraces.

6 May 1989

Two goals from Paul Moulden and one from Trevor Morley saw the Blues go in 3–0 up at half time at home to Bournemouth and on the verge of promotion. Never known to make things easy for themselves, a second-half collapse saw City crumble and in the end grateful to hold on for a point. It did leave huge question marks over their promotion hopes.

7 May 1927

Despite a superb 8–0 win over Bradford, City missed out on promotion as rivals Portsmouth beat Preston 5–1 to edge out the Blues by virtue of a marginally superior goal average.

7 May 1938

City, who had been both champions and top-scorers from the previous season were relegated after a 1–0 defeat at Huddersfield, who leapfrogged the Blues to safety in the process – along with Grimsby, Portsmouth, Birmingham and Stoke who all won on the final day of the season!

7 May 1955

Jackie Milburn scored after only 45 seconds as City were beaten 3–1 by Newcastle in the FA Cup final. Jimmy Meadows' injury had reduced the side to ten men early in the game but a brave fightback saw an equaliser early in the second half through Bobby Johnstone. However, Newcastle took advantage of tired legs and goals from Mitchell and Hannah sealed a 3–1 win for the Magpies.

7 May 1994

It was fitting that the final game of 1993/94 season ended in a draw against Sheffield Wednesday as it was the eighteenth game of Man City's campaign that ended all square – underlining almost half a season of draws.

8 May 1981

It was confirmed that winger Dave Bennett had passed a late fitness test and was expected to be named in the starting line-up for the FA Cup final against Tottenham.

8 May 1999

The 4–0 victory over York saw Nicky Weaver equal Joe Corrigan's record for the number of clean sheets in a league season with 22. Corrigan, however, appeared in 42 games, 3 less than Weaver's 45.

9 May 1981

The 100th FA Cup final, between City and Tottenham, ended in a 1–1 stalemate. City were leading 1–0 through a Tommy Hutchison header with just over 10 minutes remaining when Tottenham were awarded a free-kick twenty yards from goal. Glenn Hoddle struck the ball which Joe Corrigan looked to have covered, however, Hutchison made contact with the ball and diverted it passed Corrigan and into the net. It was a heartbreaking moment for the Blues who had battled hard throughout the game. Despite extra time being played, the sides could not be separated and the clubs would return for a replay the following Thursday.

9 May 1987

A 2–0 defeat at Upton Park against West Ham on the final day of the season dashed the Blues' slim hopes of avoiding the drop.

10 May 1968

Ahead of the vital final day of the season, concern over injuries to Colin Bell and Mike Summerbee saw them remain behind in Manchester as the rest of the squad travelled north ahead of the league championship showdown with Newcastle.

10 May 1987

Mel Machin was appointed manager following the club's relegation to the Second Division. Although the club didn't achieve promotion during his first season, Machin oversaw the introduction of many of the club's former youth team, the nucleus of which made up the side that earned promotion the following season. Despite not being considered the most successful of City managers, his win percentage in league games of almost 44 per cent is third only to Sam Cowan and Johnny Hart among post-war managers.

11 May 1968

City went into the final game of the season knowing that bettering both Liverpool and Manchester United's results would see them win their first title for over thirty years. Summerbee's opener was quickly cancelled out before Neil Young restored the lead only for Newcastle to level once again. At half time, both Liverpool and Manchester United were ahead but any nerves were quickly dispelled when Young scored just minutes into the second half. Francis Lee's strike on the hour then put the Blues two goals ahead, but with time ticking down and Blues fans beginning to celebrate, Newcastle pulled a goal back. City were not to be denied though, and the final whistle sparked joyous scenes as fans poured onto the pitch to celebrate with the title-winning side.

11 May 1981

Many fans were left disappointed after queueing all night for FA Cup final replay tickets as they did not realise that they were only being made available to season ticket holders.

11 May 1985

After stuttering the week before against Notts County, a balmy day saw City storm to a 5–1 win over Charlton to seal promotion on the final day of the season in front of a packed crowd of 47,285 at Maine Road. The Blues beat out Portsmouth on goal difference to go up with Oxford and Birmingham.

11 May 1991

A 3–2 win over relegated Sunderland on the final day of season saw City finish in fifth place. This was the club's highest league placing since finishing fourth in 1977/78, and saw them finish three points ahead of Manchester United in sixth place.

11 May 2003

The final ever game at Maine Road against Southampton drew a crowd of 34,957. A wet and rainy day saw City legends from the past paraded before the game and a gig featuring Badly Drawn Boy and Doves after the final whistle. During the game, City turned in a listless performance and fell to a 1–0 defeat, barely mustering a shot on target.

11 May 2008

The 2007/08 season that had started so promisingly was petering out amid a poor run of results and the not-so-secret news that manager Sven-Goran Eriksson was certain to get the sack. A horrendous display at the Riverside saw Richard Dunne sent off early as the club crashed to an 8–1 defeat – the club's heaviest ever Premier League defeat.

12 May 1984

City ensured bottom club Cambridge had a miserable finish to their season as the Blues ended the season in style with a 5–0 victory.

12 May 2005

Following a successful end to the season where the club narrowly missed out on qualifying for the UEFA Cup, Stuart Pearce – who had been in temporary charge following the resignation of Kevin Keegan a couple of months earlier – was handed the manager's job on a permanent basis.

13 May 1940

Four goals from Alec Herd helped defeat Crewe 6–2 in their Regional War League game at Maine Road.

13 May 1989

City headed to Valley Parade for the final game of the season knowing a point would be good enough to guarantee promotion back to Division One. However, the Blues fell behind to a Mark Ellis goal midway through the first half. Worse was to come as news filtered through from Selhurst Park that rivals Crystal Palace had raced into a heavy lead – eating away the goal difference advantage City enjoyed. With just 4 minutes remaining, and knowing a further Crystal Palace goal would knock City out of the promotion positions, Trevor Morley latched on to David White's through ball to level and earned promotion back to the top flight.

14 May 1977

A 1–0 win over Coventry at Highfield Road saw City finish second in the table behind champions Liverpool.

14 May 1981

City fell to a pair of goals from Ricky Villa in a 3–2 FA Cup final replay defeat that went down as one of the greatest finals of all-time. After falling behind early, Steve Mackenzie's wonder strike levelled matters before Kevin Reeves' penalty put the Blues in front. The Blues were to be denied, though, as Garth Crooks hit home from close range and just 5 minutes later Villa jinked his way through the defence before lifting the ball over Joe Corrigan to break Blues' hearts.

14 May 1983

Just two years after losing a Wembley cup final, a 1–0 defeat against Luton saw the Hatters survive at City's expense. The Blues needed just a point from the game and looked to have done enough in a nervy game but with only 5 minutes remaining Raddy Antic sensationally struck for Luton. Full time saw Luton manager David Pleat dance a jig across Maine Road and the result meant City went into the bottom three for the first time during the whole of the 1982/83 season.

14 May 2007

Amid growing rumours of a takeover by former Thai Prime Minister Thaksin Shinawatra, manager Stuart Pearce was sacked at the end of a disappointing season. Pearce had struggled to take the side forward with the financial constraints the club had, and was clearly envious of the potential riches his replacement may have to spend, saying 'the previous manager had around £50m to spend and if the club is taken over the next manager may have £50m . . . in that sense I feel I have been a caretaker with no money to spend, getting the books balanced while keeping them in the Premiership.'

15 May 1999

Paul Dickov equalised to make the final score 1–1 after falling behind to a goal against Wigan in the first minute of the Divison Two play-off semi-final first leg.

15 May 2005

Nicky Weaver was brought on in goal with keeper David James pushed up front in attack for the last few minutes as City searched for the winner against Middlesbrough that would have seen the club qualify for the UEFA Cup. James' presence caused plenty of problems and he was fouled, winning a last-minute penalty. However, Robbie Fowler missed the resulting spot kick and the game ended 1–1 with the Blues finishing in eighth position.

16 May 1995

Brian Horton's difficult time as manager of the club came to an end as after months of speculation, chairman Francis Lee finally pulled the plug on his reign. Despite mixed results and a pair of relegation battles, Horton's sides were known for playing attacking and entertaining football, but having not been Lee's appointment, he was always on borrowed time.

17 May 1892

Ardwick AFC were elected as founder members of Football League Division Two.

18 May 1966

Already crowned as Division Two champions, a largely uneventful 0–0 draw was played out with Southampton at Maine Road to end the season.

19 May 1937

City became the first English side to play at Berlin's Olympic Stadium as part of the end of season tour. The Blues put in a brave performance but were defeated 3–2 by the German national side who were keen to impress the watching nation.

19 May 1999

Shaun Goater scored the only goal in the play-off second leg at home to Wigan to send City to Wembley thanks to a 2–1 aggregate win.

19 May 2007

Former Thai Prime Minister Thaksin Shinawatra made a formal offer to buy the club. Although stressing that a deal had not been concluded, Thaksin's lawyer Noppadon Pattama said, 'The deal is not formally or legally concluded yet. What I can say now is we have tendered a bid for the team. We had to be silent because we had to follow the stock market regulations as we are trying to buy a listed company.'

20 May 1987

Defensive pillar Mick McCarthy left the club following the relegation season to join Scottish side Celtic who were looking to strengthen after seeing rivals Rangers win the Scottish Premier Division the previous season.

21 May 2001

Following successive promotions, life was always going to be tough for City to survive in the Premier League and despite battling bravely, the club slipped to relegation, perhaps not ready to step up so quickly. Feeling that Joe Royle had taken the side as far as he could, the club dismissed him following the conclusion of the season. A bitter dispute followed between Royle and the club, centred around at the time of his sacking whether the club were still technically classed as a Premier League side.

22 May 1973

City player and Australian international Danny Tiatto was born. Tiatto arrived at Maine Road from Swiss side FC Baden in 1997 and the combative and versatile player spent five seasons at the club, playing 159 times before moving on to Leicester.

23 May 2001

Just two days after Joe Royle's sacking, Kevin Keegan was appointed as City boss. Under his stewardship the club immediately bounced back with a season of fast-flowing and attacking football. Following promotion, Keegan spent wisely and the club consolidated itself in the top flight, but some ill-judged forays into the transfer market stalled the club's progress and the energy that Keegan brought at the start of his time in charge ebbed away before he stepped down in March 2005.

24 May 1941

An interesting feature of the Regional Wartime leagues was the high-scoring nature of the games. City's game against Bolton was no exception as Jackie Currier's hat-trick helped the club to an entertaining 6–4 win.

24 May 1947

Les McDowall and George Smith both hit goals in the 2–0 victory over West Ham at Upton Park.

25 May 2009

Abu Dhabi-based airline Etihad were announced as the
new shirt sponsor, replacing travel firm Thomas Cook.

26 May 2006

Paul Dickov re-signed for the club following his release
from Blackburn. Dickov had been the Wembley hero
some seven years earlier, and while he remained a popular
player, his signing was indicative of the lack of resources
available at the club at the time.

27 May 1937

Speaking at the end of the club's end of season tour
to Germany, captain Sam Barkas said, 'I am not going
to pretend that English football teams making tours of
Continental countries do not have a very pleasant time, but
at the same time these tours are not picnics. You are there
to play serious football, and you have to go about it in the
ordinary businesslike way.'

28 May 2009

After back-to-back impressive seasons, Stephen Ireland penned a new contract at the club, believed to be worth in the region of £60,000 per week.

29 May 1949

Future City player and coach Brian Kidd was born. Kidd had been part of the successful side in the late 1960s but joined City from Arsenal in 1976. The forward scored 57 goals in 128 games before signing for Everton. After a number of coaching spells and having held the manager's position at Blackburn, Kidd returned to the club as an assistant to Roberto Mancini when the Italian replaced Mark Hughes.

30 May 1999

Dead and buried at 2–0 down and heading into injury time in the Division Two play-off final against Gillingham, City staged arguably the most dramatic and important comeback in the club's history. With 6 minutes' injury time signalled, Kevin Horlock grabbed what appeared to be nothing more than a consolation goal, but with fans having left the stadium in droves, Paul Dickov struck an improbable equaliser to shatter Gillingham hearts. Extra time produced no further goals and the game moved to the dreaded penalty shoot-out. Despite goal hero Dickov missing City's second penalty, Gillingham failed to convert their first two. Nicky Weaver then saved Gillingham's fourth penalty to win promotion and kick off the celebrations.

31 May 1906

The punishment was handed down to the players and officials who were investigated following allegations that Billy Meredith offered Aston Villa's Alec Leake £10 to throw a game between the two sides. The decision that was announced saw seventeen players and officials from the club suspended until the following January.

June

1 June 1925

Future City player Roy Clarke was born. Clarke was a long-time Blue, making his debut in 1947 and he played for the club 370 times winning an FA Cup winner's medal in 1956. After hanging up his boots, Clarke became the first manager of the City Social Club and remained close to the club up until his death in 2006.

1 June 1950

Les McDowall took over the club following relegation to Division Two. He had been a player of some note at the end of the 1930s, but his tenure as manager was even more successful. Promotion was achieved at the first time of asking and McDowall added notable names such as Roy Paul and Don Revie to the club, later introducing the formation known as the 'Revie Plan' to great success as the side won the FA Cup in 1956. However, as football progressed in the 1960s it was felt that the Scot had not moved with the times and the club suffered relegation at the end of the 1962/63 season, ending McDowall's time in charge.

2 June 1970

Francis Lee played as England defeated Romania 1–0 in their group clash in the 1970 World Cup finals.

2 June 2003

The club were notified that they had been awarded a place in the 2003/04 UEFA Cup due via the Fair Play route as a result of England topping the UEFA rankings.

2 June 2008

After being in limbo towards the end of the season, even remaining in charge for the club's post-season tour to Thailand, Sven-Goran Eriksson was sacked as manager. Ultimately the decision was not a surprise given the rampant speculation about his future, but the move was considered hasty given the strides the Swede had made during his solitary season in charge.

3 June 1972

Having 'moved upstairs' the previous October, enabling Malcolm Allison to take sole charge of the playing side of the club, Joe Mercer left his position as general manager to join Coventry City, ending his long and successful association with the club.

3 June 1978

Asa Hartford played in Scotland's 3–1 defeat to Peru in their group game in the World Cup finals.

4 June 2002

The 2–0 win for Costa Rica over China in the World Cup finals saw City players Sun Jihai and Paulo Wanchope go head to head.

4 June 2003

City signed veteran Arsenal goalkeeper David Seaman to replace the recently retired Peter Schmeichel.

4 June 2008

Mark Hughes was appointed as manager to replace Sven-Goran Eriksson. The former Manchester United player struggled to win over fans during his time in charge, and his first season at the club resulted in underachievement in the league and domestic cup competitions, but they did progress to the last eight of the UEFA Cup. The following summer saw Hughes spend huge sums and revamp the look of the squad, but despite being well-placed in the league at the end of 2009, Hughes was sacked and replaced with Roberto Mancini.

5 June 1986

Midfielder David Phillips moved to Coventry for a fee of £150,000 with goalkeeper Perry Suckling moving in the opposite direction.

5 June 1913

Future City player Peter Doherty was born. No less a person than Danny Blanchflower called him the greatest player he had ever seen. Doherty was signed for a then record £10,000 in February 1936 and scored 81 times for the club in just 133 appearances. Following the war, Doherty moved to Derby and would later manage Northern Ireland.

6 June 2002

The club shattered its transfer record with the £13.5 million signing of Nicolas Anelka from PSG. Anelka had earned a reputation as a petulant character (he was given the moniker 'le Sulk') from his time at Arsenal and Real Madrid. During his spell at the club – the longest time he had spent at any one club at the time – the French striker scored an impressive 45 goals in 101 games before being sold to Turkish side Fenerbahce.

7 June 1970

Colin Bell came on as a second-half substitute in England's 1–0 World Cup group game defeat to Brazil. Fellow Blue Francis Lee started the match.

7 June 1971

In a three-way fight along with Crystal Palace and Coventry, City refused to increase their bid of £140,000 for Rodney Marsh with Joe Mercer saying, 'We believed it was realistic and as far as we could go. The amount of money involved is tremendous when examined coldly. One deal like this could ruin a club for years to come.' It was a move criticised by Peter Gardner in the *Manchester Evening News* who felt that the club could easily have recouped the outlay with the additional gate receipts the signing would have generated.

7 June 1978

Both Asa Hartford and Willie Donachie played in Scotland's disastrous showing against Peru in the World Cup that ended in a 1–1 draw.

8 June 1928

Future player, manager and long-time club stalwart Johnny Hart was born in Golborne on this day.

9 June 1958

City's post-season tour to the USA was brought to a successful conclusion with the club remaining unbeaten throughout their travels.

9 June 1988

Rugged central defender Brian Gayle was brought in from Wimbledon for a fee of £250,000. Gayle would become a captain of the club during his time at Maine Road before moving on to Ipswich in 1990.

10 June 1957

Two-time Blue Peter Barnes was born. The son of former
player and scout Ken Barnes, Peter was brought through
the ranks at the club and made his debut aged just
seventeen in 1974, going on to win the PFA Young Player
of the Year award in 1976. Barnes was a hugely popular
player at the club but was sold against his wishes by
Malcolm Allison as he broke up the side during his second
spell in charge. Barnes would return to the club in 1987
for a brief spell during the club's relegation season. In total,
Barnes made 149 starts for the club and scored 22 goals.

11 June 1970

Colin Bell started for England in their 1–0 win over
Czechoslovakia in the final group game at the World Cup
finals, a result that saw England progress to the knock-out
stages.

11 June 1978

Asa Hartford and Willie Donachie both played in
Scotland's 3–2 win over Holland – a game that despite
resulting in Scotland exiting the World Cup was famous for
Archie Gemmill's solo wonder goal.

11 June 1992

Classy central defender Keith Curle was played in an
unfamiliar right-back spot for England in their 0–0 draw in
the opening group game of the tournament against France.

12 June 1972

The *Manchester Evening News* reported that the City board
wanted to strip Joe Mercer of his title as manager and leave
Malcolm Allison in sole charge.

12 June 1986

Sammy McIlroy played in the 3–0 defeat to Brazil as
Northern Ireland crashed out of the World Cup finals in
Mexico.

13 June 1975

Mike Summerbee's City career came to an end as he was
sold to Burnley for a transfer fee of £25,000. Summerbee
was one of the key parts of the famous City side in the
late 1960s and early 1970s and also won eight England
caps. Summerbee later went on to be player-manager of

Stockport but always maintained strong links with the Blues and in 2009 was announced as a club ambassador.

13 June 2002

Paulo Wanchope was on the scoresheet but Costa Rica fell to a 5–2 defeat against Brazil in the World Cup finals.

13 June 2006

The club announced that they were planning a huge revamp of their Junior Blues Club later that summer. Pioneered in the 1970s, the Junior Blues was the biggest scheme of its type with over 8,000 members and it became a model for many other clubs.

14 June 1947

George Smith scored all five in City's 5–1 victory over Newport which was the latest ever finish to a season due to the disruption that the weather had caused during the campaign.

14 June 1970

Francis Lee started in England's famous 3–2 defeat to West Germany in the World Cup quarter-final, despite racing out to an early two-goal lead. Fellow Blue Colin Bell was introduced as a second-half substitute in the game.

15 June 1972

After being handed a new 'upstairs' role that he appeared to initially accept, Joe Mercer left the club to take charge of Coventry with a parting shot at the board, saying, 'The humiliating part of this sad affair is that at one time the board were saying there was a job for life. But the new regime had no real confidence in me and I ended up with a three-year contract and a 33 per cent cut in salary.'

16 June 1982

Trevor Francis played in England's 3–1 win in the group opener against France at the World Cup finals, a game famous for Bryan Robson's opening goal after just 27 seconds.

17 June 2009

The 2009/10 fixtures were released and saw the Blues handed a trip to Mark Hughes' former club Blackburn on the opening day of the season.

18 June 1994

Full-back Terry Phelan played in Ireland's famous 1–0 win over Italy at USA '94, a result that helped them qualify for the knock-out stages.

18 June 2010

Gareth Barry returned from injury to the England side, but their disappointing opening to the World Cup continued with a 0–0 draw against Algeria.

19 June 2008

The Blues looked to be in a position to make a serious bid for Ronaldinho – who was surplus to requirements at Barcelona – as AC Milan appeared to distance themselves from him.

20 June 1982

Trevor Francis was on the scoresheet in England's 2–0
win over Czechoslovakia in their clash at the World Cup
group stage.

20 June 2001

One of the first moves Kevin Keegan made in charge was
the signing of Stuart Pearce. Although thirty-nine years
of age, Pearce's experience and influence was heavily
relied upon as Keegan sought to steer the club back into
the Premier League. Although Pearce only played for one
season at the club, after hanging up his boots he joined the
coaching set-up and later took charge of the side following
the departure of Keegan.

21 June 1988

After failing to gain promotion to the top flight, forward
Paul Stewart moved to Tottenham for a fee of £1.7 million.

21 June 1990

Niall Quinn scored for Ireland in their 1–1 draw against
Holland at Italia '90.

22 June 1994

Nicky Summerbee signed from Swindon for a fee of
£1.5 million, following the same route to the club that
his father Mike had taken three decades earlier. Despite
being a talented winger, Summerbee struggled to escape
the shadow of the legacy his father had created and never
quite won over the supporters, and after making 156
appearances he signed for Sunderland in 1997 in a
£1 million move.

23 June 1937

Scotsman Bobby Kennedy was born. Kennedy was signed
from Kilmarnock for £45,000 in the summer of 1961 and
made over 250 appearances for the club before becoming
player-manager of Grimsby in 1968.

24 June 1986

City played a friendly against Scottish side Dundee in
San José, winning 5–4 on penalties.

25 June 1982

Trevor Francis netted for the second game in succession at the World Cup finals as England ran out 1–0 victors over Kuwait in their final group game.

25 June 1990

Niall Quinn played for Ireland as Pat Bonner's penalty save sent the Irish through to the quarter-finals on penalties after their encounter against Romania finished goalless at the end of extra time.

26 June 1979

Dave Watson was sold to Werder Bremen as Malcolm Allison looked to continue to overhaul the squad during his second spell in charge. Watson – an England international – was an all-action player who was a cult hero on the terraces, and his departure left a huge hole in defence that the club failed to adequately fill for many years.

26 June 1987

Brother were announced as the new shirt sponsor, replacing Saab, whose five-year deal had come to an end.

The Japanese company had a long and fruitful partnership with the club, spanning just over a decade in total.

26 June 2003

Signed by Kevin Keegan in the summer of 2002 from French side Lyon following the club's promotion back to the Premier League, Marc-Vivien Foe was an integral part of the side that finished ninth on their return to the top flight. The following summer, Foe represented Cameroon in the Confederations Cup and during their semi-final game against Colombia, he collapsed in the centre-circle. After attempts to resuscitate him on the pitch, Foe was stretchered from the field. Medics spent a desperate 45 minutes attempting to revive him, and although he was still alive upon arrival at the stadium's medical centre, he died shortly afterwards. An autopsy would conclude that his death was heart-related. Foe was just twenty-eight years old.

27 June 1986

Stalwart Paul Power moved to Everton for a £65,000 fee. After making his debut in 1975, Power soon became a key member of City's left-hand side and would go on to captain the side in the 1981 FA Cup final against Tottenham. Despite the club's relegation in 1983, he opted to stay and help them back to the top flight in 1985. He signed for Everton a year later, going on to win a championship medal with the Merseysiders. In total, Power made 447 appearances for the club and later returned to City to work with the academy.

27 June 2003

Following the death of Marc-Vivien Foe, City announced that the number 23 that Foe wore at the club would be retired, meaning that no other player would wear that shirt again.

28 June 1967

The club caused unrest among supporters after announcing ticket price rises of up to 20 per cent in some sections of the ground.

29 June 1982

Trevor Francis was replaced late in England's 0–0 draw with West Germany in the second group stage of the World Cup finals.

30 June 1947

Sam Cowan stepped down as City manager after just seven months in charge. Cowan had been captain of the side during the 1930s and the decision to appoint him was warmly greeted. His arrival as manager bore instant success and the club lost only four of the thirty games after he took over. However, there was friction off the field as Cowan came into conflict with chairman Robert Smith and he felt he could no longer continue, saying, 'Something happened, and I felt that I had no option but to hand in my resignation. I don't want to implicate anyone, so rather than cause any trouble I would prefer to leave the matter there.'

30 June 1983

Former Celtic manager Billy McNeill was appointed as manager as the club looked to bounce back from the disappointment of relegation to Division Two. The appointment of McNeill was a statement that despite relegation, the club's standing was still such that it could attract a top calibre of manager. After a season of consolidation, McNeill guided the club to promotion in 1985 but a year later stunned everyone as he walked out on City to take charge of Aston Villa – a decision which saw him become the first manager to be in charge of two relegated sides as both City and Villa dropped out of the top flight.

30 June 1995

To the disappointment of most supporters, Alan Ball was appointed as manager. Rumours of names such as George Graham had been circulating but Francis Lee turned to his old friend Ball to be the man to take the Blues forward. The club started the 1995/96 season poorly, not registering their first win until November and were relegated on the final day of the season. Ball was backed by Francis Lee, but after a 2–1 defeat to Stoke at the start of the following season, amid growing supporter unrest, Ball and the club parted company.

July

1 July 1940

Future City player George Heslop was born. The defender arrived at the club from Everton in 1965 and was part of the side that won the league, League Cup and European Cup Winners' Cup over the next few seasons.

2 July 1998

After over a decade of service and 337 appearances for the club, the versatile Ian Brightwell moved on to Coventry City on a free transfer, the last of the 'Boy Blues' who had come through the youth team ranks in the mid-1980s.

2 July 2008

Brazilian striker Jo arrived from Russian side CSKA for a club record fee of £19 million. Although a Mark Hughes signing, the transfer had been orchestrated by the previous regime. Arriving with a big reputation, he showed occasional flashes of brilliance early in the season but Hughes quickly tired of his inconsistencies and the player was farmed out to both Everton and Galatasaray on loan.

2 July 2010

Yaya Toure was officially confirmed as a Manchester City player following his move from Barcelona for a reported fee of £28 million. The *News of The World* would later report that Toure would be earning up to £200,000 per week.

3 July 2003

Mexican Matias Vuoso was loaned out to Santos Laguna in his home nation. A Kevin Keegan signing – reportedly for £3.5 million – he failed to feature in a single first-team game in the previous 13 months at the club. He was later given a free transfer having never pulled on a City shirt.

4 July 1938

Harry Dowd was born in Salford. Dowd joined the club as an amateur and succeeded Bert Trautmann between the posts and remained first choice for most of his career, although he missed out on the majority of the league winning season of 1967/68. He did, however, win back his place the following season and was in goal for the 1969 FA Cup final win. After making 219 appearances for the club, Dowd transferred to Oldham in December 1970.

4 July 1994

Terry Phelan played as Ireland crashed out 2–0 to Holland in the last sixteen of the World Cup at USA '94. Fellow City defender Alan Kernaghan was an unused substitute.

4 July 2002

The club signed Sylvain Distin from French side PSG for £4 million. Distin had spent the previous season on loan at Newcastle and quickly established himself as an important player at the club. A smooth, classy defender, he built up an excellent partnership with Richard Dunne which was the bedrock of the side during the mid-part of the decade but mysteriously failed to earn international recognition. With uncertainty off the pitch at the club growing, Distin ran down his contract and signed for Portsmouth in the summer of 2007.

5 July 1982

Trevor Francis could not find the scoresheet as England drew 0–0 with Spain to exit the World Cup at the second group phase following two successive goalless draws.

5 July 2007

After leaving the club to join Championship side Charlton, Nicky Weaver hit out at the club. Weaver had fought back from injury to win back the starting role but after the club stalled on offering a new deal, he said, 'I was told the contract offered while Stuart Pearce was manager was no longer on the table and I would have to basically go on trial for the new manager. I found that a bit of an insult, given that I played more than 30 games last season. My agent made it clear I didn't want to leave City, where I had spent most of my adult life, but in the end it became clear it was time to move on.'

6 July 1973

Crowd hero Gio Kinkladze was born in Tbilisi. A player with immense talent and natural ability, he quickly endeared himself to supporters with his displays in a struggling side and remarkably remained with the club through two relegations, such was the depth of his feeling.

Despite making only 122 appearances, there are not many players of modern times remembered with such devotion.

6 July 2007

Former England manager Sven-Goran Eriksson was appointed as manager as Thaksin Shinawatra's takeover of the club was all but completed. It was to be the Swede's first position since leaving the England post and he quickly assembled a side in little over a month, bringing in almost a dozen new players to signal a new air of positivity at the club.

7 July 1958

Gary Owen was born. The winger progressed through the youth ranks to make his debut in 1976 and although he missed out on a League Cup final berth, he became a regular the following season and won England under-21 and B caps during his time at Maine Road before being controversially sold to West Brom by Malcolm Allison.

8 July 2009

In an interview with the *Manchester Evening News*, Garry Cook ruffled some feathers among supporters by declaring he wanted to do away with the phrase 'City 'Til I Die', believing it to be connected with years of underachievement at the club.

9 July 2008

Former chairman John Wardle announced that he had stepped down from his position as deputy chairman and also from the board of directors.

10 July 1927

Future City player Don Revie was born in Middlesbrough.

11 July 2005

Arsenal manager Arsene Wenger confirmed his interest in winger Shaun Wright-Phillips, but admitted that he would have to wait until Chelsea first showed their hand, saying, 'I like Wright-Phillips very much, but we are in a transfer market where you first have to let Chelsea make decisions, then come in when they have made that decision. That is because there is a price for Chelsea and a price for everybody else.'

11 July 2010

Nigel de Jong became the first City player to feature in a World Cup final as he started for the Netherlands in the 1–0 defeat at the hands of Spain. De Jong's performance was notable for a high, studs-up challenge on Xabi Alonso that earned him a yellow card. David Silva – whom it was announced would join the Blues after the World Cup – was on the bench for Spain, but wasn't called into action.

12 July 1963

In replacing Les McDowall, the club opted for his former assistant, George Poyser. Poyser's background was more in the scouting department and was perhaps never quite suited to be the 'main man'. His first season brought a sixth-place finish and a semi-final appearance in the League Cup but the following season saw the side struggle and Poyser was replaced at Easter 1965.

12 July 1990

Watford goalkeeper Tony Coton was signed for a fee of £1 million. Coton had built a solid career at Birmingham and Watford before arriving at the club and very quickly proved to be a solid signing. Coton was named as the fans' player of the year in 1993/94, yet despite his consistent displays, England recognition somehow eluded him.

13 July 1965

Joe Mercer was appointed as manager, a decision that would be the catalyst for the club's golden period over the following decade. A player of some repute for both Everton and Arsenal, Mercer had managed at Aston Villa but stepped down due to health issues. However, following a year out of the game, he was tempted back into management when the City job became available. On arriving at Maine Road, Mercer was keen to not inflate hopes, saying there would be 'no rash promises, no gimmicks.'

14 July 1996

Former captain Keith Curle signed for Wolves in a £650,000 move, continuing the purge of the higher earners at the club following relegation from the Premier League.

15 July 1995

The club confirmed the signing of Gio Kinkladze. The diminutive Georgian was brought to the club by Francis Lee on the eve of the 1995/96 season, leaving Alan Ball to proclaim that he would have fans 'hanging from the rafters.' His rapport with the fans was strong – perhaps much too strong as he decided to continue with the club following relegation but suffered as the supporting cast around him was not good. The arrival of Joe Royle signalled the end of his time at the club as he was cast adrift with the club slipping into the third tier. For most fans, though, he brought a rare ray of light during an otherwise gloomy spell in the club's history.

16 July 1979

Malcolm Allison returned to the club for a second spell in charge. The club had enjoyed a relatively successful season and Chairman Peter Swales felt that the return of Allison would be the move to put the club over the edge. Allison, however, couldn't replicate the success of his first spell in charge and was sacked just over a year later.

17 July 1976

The long and successful playing career of Alan Oakes ended when he signed for Chester City in a deal worth £15,000 that would see him take the reins as player-manager. Thought of by a succession of managers as the ultimate professional, Oakes would ultimately make 680 appearances for City, a record unlikely ever to be beaten.

17 July 2005

Shaun Wright-Phillips was sold to Chelsea for a club record fee of £21 million. Wright-Phillips had battled through the ranks and flourished during Kevin Keegan's time in charge into an England international. During a lean time at the club, Wright-Phillips was often a lone bright spot but with Chelsea's millions on offer the fee was too good for the club to turn down given their financial position.

18 July 1989

Having been promoted to the First Division, manager Mel Machin sought to add both experience and goals to the squad in the shape of Clive Allen, who arrived in a £1 million move from Bordeaux. Upon signing Allen said, 'I have no doubt in my mind that Man City are going places, and I want to go with then.' Allen started brightly, but suffered frustrating injuries and when Howard Kendall took over he found himself out of favour. In 1991 he moved on to Chelsea, having scored 16 goals in 31 starts.

18 July 1992

City defeated a League of Ireland XI 3–0 in a pre-season friendly but saw goalkeeper Andy Dibble suffer a broken leg in the process.

19 July 2008

The Blues travelled to the Faroe Islands to kick off their season with a UEFA Cup qualifying tie against EB/Streymur, emerging victorious with a comfortable 2–0 victory in what was Mark Hughes' first game in charge.

20 July 1966

City signed thirty-year-old Tony Book from Plymouth. The signing was mainly inspired by Malcolm Allison who had Book at the Pilgrims and decided to sign him for £17,000. He would become a key member of the side until the early 1970s, making 312 appearances for the club and winning a number of trophies in the process.

21 July 1965

One of the first moves that new manager Joe Mercer made was to appoint a young coach named Malcolm Allison as his assistant. The decision would prove to be a wise one and instrumental in helping shape the side that achieved such success over the next decade.

21 July 1977

Southampton directors were in talks to decide whether to accept the £250,000 bid that City had made for Mick Channon or to insist on a player-plus-cash deal instead.

22 July 2005

Joey Barton was sent home from the club's pre-season tour to Thailand after an altercation with a fifteen-year-old Everton fan that also saw Barton in a dispute with captain Richard Dunne.

23 July 2009

The *Mail* reported that Daniel Sturridge was all set to leave the club after his contract expired and move to Chelsea with a fee being set by a tribunal.

24 July 1979

The club were rumoured to be considering an offer for playmakers Dejan Stepanovic and Ronald Aman should the pursuit of Wolves midfielder Steve Daley have proved unsuccessful.

25 July 2005

The club announced the signing of Aston Villa's England striker Darius Vassell for a reported fee of £2.5 million.

25 July 2007

Thai defenders Suree Sukha and Kiatprawut Saiwaeo and striker Teerasil Dangda were all taken on trial by the club in a move that was widely suggested was a direct result of Thaksin Shinawatra gaining control of the club.

26 July 1985

The *Manchester Evening News* reported that eighteen-year-old youth team prospect Earl Barrett was expected to make his debut for the club in the forthcoming season opener against Coventry City, with Billy McNeill saying of the teenager, 'He impressed all the backroom staff last season.'

26 July 2007

City announced the signing of Bulgarian winger Martin Petrov from Atletico Madrid for a fee of £4.7 million.

27 July 1972

Mike Summerbee was fined £150 by the FA and warned about his future conduct after accumulating three cautions inside a year.

27 July 1972

Speaking to the press, Colin Bell said he believed that Rodney Marsh, 'needs twenty or so games to come good.'

28 July 2005

Former Blues Frank Swift, Bert Trautmann, Francis Lee
and Colin Bell made the final seventy-five list of potential
inductees into the Football Hall of Fame. Managerial duo
Joe Mercer and Malcolm Allison were named in the fifteen-
strong managerial category.

29 July 2009

The protracted and bitter transfer saga with Everton over
the club's desire to sign Joleon Lescott continued as Sky
Sports reported that an increased offer from the initial
£15 million one that was rejected would shortly be made.

30 July 1874

Billy Meredith was born. Meredith spent two spells at
the club either side of playing at Manchester United. The
Welshman scored 146 league goals to cement his place
as one of the all-time greats. Off the field, Meredith did
much for his fellow players in setting up an early version
of the Professional Footballers' Association and after his
body had spent many years in an unmarked grave, the PFA,
the Welsh FA and both City and Manchester United, in a

tribute to his influence on the modern game, all agreed to cover the cost of the upkeep on a new headstone.

30 July 1991

Reserve team player Ashley Ward was allowed to leave the club after just three substitute appearances, moving to Crewe for a nominal fee. The move continued a trend of the previous few seasons where young players moved on, only to go on to establish themselves back in the top flight and often command big transfer fees. Notable other examples of ones who slipped through the net include Neil Lennon, Paul Warhurst and Earl Barrett.

31 July 1997

The club signed Lee Bradbury for £3 million to bolster their strikeforce ahead of the new season. The former solider arrived from Portsmouth with a good goalscoring record from the previous season but could never get going for the Blues and quickly became a target for the fans. Bradbury would depart for Crystal Palace after scoring just eleven goals for the club.

August

1 August 2009

The *News of the World* reported that the recent big-money signings made by Mark Hughes had seen the club's wage bill rise in excess of £100 million per season.

2 August 1969

City were defeated 2–1 by Leeds in the annual Charity Shield curtain-raiser at Wembley.

2 August 1975

Dave Watson made his debut for Man City against Blackpool in the Anglo-Scottish Cup after joining the club from Sunderland.

2 August 2000

On the eve of the new season, newly promoted City pulled off a coup as they announced the signing of former World Footballer of the Year, George Weah. There were high hopes for the Liberian but Weah did not even last the full season and departed the club after scoring just once in the Premier League.

3 August 1968

League winners from the previous season, a confident City comfortably opened the new season with a 6–1 victory over West Brom at Maine Road in the Charity Shield.

4 August 1987

The two-day Manchester International Football Tournament got under way at Maine Road. City were defeated by Manchester United but bounced back to beat PSV Eindhoven to finish third in the inaugural tournament.

5 August 1972

A penalty from Francis Lee was enough to defeat Aston Villa in the Charity Shield. The game was only contested between the two sides after league champions Derby County and FA Cup winners Leeds United had declined to take part.

5 August 1989

Summer signings Clive Allen and Ian Bishop made their first appearances for the club in the pre-season friendly against Port Vale.

6 August 1991

City made Keith Curle the most expensive British defender after signing him from Wimbledon for a fee of £2.5 million. The future captain would go on to make over 200 appearances for the club before moving to Wolves.

7 August 1993

In a controversial move, the club appointed former journalist John Maddock to a newly created General

Manager role at the club. Maddock didn't have a great deal of credentials to be qualified for the position but was tasked with reviewing the current state of the playing side of the club.

8 August 1998

City opened the season in the third tier of English football in front of a crowd of 32,134 with a 3–0 win over Blackpool via goals from Goater, Bradbury and Tskhadadze.

9 August 1914

Joe Mercer was born. The greatest and most successful City manager of all time, Mercer presided over an unparalleled period of success for the club for just short of a decade. Always conducting himself with his trademark warmth and humility, his teams were well known for their attractive style of football. He also managed Aston Villa and Coventry and acted as England caretaker manager. Mercer also passed away on this date, on his seventy-sixth birthday in 1990.

9 August 1997

The 2–2 draw at home to Portsmouth on the opening day of the 1997/98 season saw City sport a new kit, made by Kappa and also a new club badge. The new shield design featured a ship on its upper half representing the Manchester Ship Canal, and three diagonal stripes in the lower half denoting the city's rivers. The motto *'Superbia in Proelio'* also featured in addition to three stars placed at the top of the badge.

9 August 2000

The club again broke their transfer record by signing Paulo Wanchope from West Ham for £3.65 million. The unpredictable Costa Rican spent four years at the club, averaging around a goal every two starts before moving to Spanish side Malaga.

10 August 1968

Neil Young scored in the 2–1 defeat to Liverpool as the club opened the defence of its league title at Anfield.

10 August 2003

Trevor Sinclair netted the winner as the club opened the new City of Manchester Stadium with a 2–1 friendly win over a Barcelona side featuring World Player of the Year Ronaldinho.

11 August 2001

A goal from debutant Stuart Pearce capped a convincing 3–0 win over Watford at Maine Road to begin Kevin Keegan's time in charge.

12 August 1997

City's dismal run of cup results against lower-league opposition continued as they fell 1–0 to Blackpool in the first leg of their Coca-Cola Cup second round clash.

13 August 1974

Scottish midfielder Asa Hartford was signed from West Brom for a fee of £210,000.

14 August 1974

After 384 total appearances and 148 goals for the club, Francis Lee joined Derby in a £110,000 move. Perhaps proving that it was a mistake to sell him on at just thirty years of age, Lee won the league title in his very first season at Derby – just like he had done for City back in 1968.

14 August 2003

A crowd of 34,103 witnessed the first competitive game at the City of Manchester Stadium as the Blues comfortably defeated Welsh side TNS 5–0 in the first leg of their UEFA Cup first round qualifier.

15 August 1987

The opening day victory over Plymouth was reportedly the first game to witness an inflatable banana on the Maine Road terraces.

15 August 1996

In continuing the purge of the more experienced and higher-earning players following the club's relegation, Irish international Niall Quinn was sold to Sunderland for £1.3 million. Quinn achieved cult hero status during his years at the club, a feeling that was replicated following his move to Wearside.

15 August 1997

City were the first visitors to Sunderland's Stadium of Light. The Blues slipped to a 3–1 defeat with Niall Quinn opening the scoring for the home side.

15 August 2007

A Michael Johnson goal gave City a 1–0 win over newly promoted Derby in the opening home game of the season. It was the first goal in nine home games, after the final eight games of the previous season had failed to yield a goal following the 2–1 win over Everton on New Year's Day. In all, during 2006/07 only 29 goals were scored in 38 games, with just 10 coming at the City of Manchester Stadium.

16 August 1969

The club's sticky start to the season continued as they were defeated 1–0 away at Newcastle.

17 August 1968

The first Manchester derby of the season pitted the league champions against the European Cup winners, but a negative display from United saw the game end in a goalless draw.

17 August 1974

The Blues kicked off the season in style with a convincing 4–0 win over West Ham with two of the goals coming from Rodney Marsh.

17 August 1992

The 1992/93 season saw the club kick off the new Premier League as part of Sky TV's Monday night football. The coverage featured cheerleaders, fireworks and dancing girls as David White's goal earned City a 1–1 draw at home to QPR. The game also saw Paul Lake's first game back after injury and playing in a more advanced midfield role.

18 August 1962

City opened the 1961/62 in disastrous fashion as they were hammered 8–1 at Molineux by Wolves on the opening day of the season.

18 August 1971

Francis Lee scored the first of thirteen penalties of the season in the 4–0 victory over Crystal Palace.

19 August 1901

Tommy Johnson was born. Johnson became an idol at the club during the 1920s thanks to his goalscoring exploits and to this day, his tally of 38 league goals in 1928/29 remains a club record. During his eleven years with the Blues he netted a total of 158 league goals – the most in City history.

19 August 1992

With high hopes following his return to the side at the start of the season, tragedy struck for Paul Lake as he was stretchered off at Middlesbrough with a recurrence of the knee injury that had kept him out for so long. The 2–0 defeat at Ayresome Park would prove to be the final game he would play for the club. Niall Quinn was also sent off during the game, becoming the first City player to receive his marching orders since the inception of the Premier League.

19 August 1998

City beat Notts County 7–1 in their Coca-Cola Cup first round tie. Popular duo Paul Dickov and Shaun Goater grabbed a brace apiece as the Blues went through 9–1 on aggregate.

19 August 2007

The 1–0 victory over Manchester United saw Kasper Schmeichel make his only derby appearance, remaining unbeaten in Manchester derbies like his father Peter, who of course played with distinction for both United and City.

20 August 1949

With regular goalkeeper Alec Thurlow suffering from health troubles, legendary figure Frank Swift came out of retirement to play in City's 3–3 home draw against Aston Villa.

21 August 1965

Glyn Pardoe became the first player to be named as a substitute for City on the opening day of 1965/66 season after the Football League decided to permit substitutions.

However, the honour of the first substitute to be used fell to Roy Cheetham who replaced Mike Summerbee nine days later in the 4–2 victory over Wolves.

21 August 1979

After bravely battling through injury to get back into the City side, Colin Bell announced his retirement after admitting defeat in his bid to recapture his pre-injury fitness and form. Upon hanging up his boots, Chairman Peter Swales described Bell as 'irreplaceable'.

22 August 1953

The first home game of the campaign was a disappointing one as City crashed to the eventual Champions Wolves 4–0.

22 August 1996

Arriving from Arsenal in a £750,000 move, Paul Dickov became Alan Ball's final signing before departing the club. Dickov put the off-field uncertainty behind him and his all-action style quickly endeared him to fans. Although part of the side that slipped to the third tier, Dickov played his part in helping the club return to the top flight and of course will be forever synonomous with the club's resurrection after scoring *that* goal at Wembley in 1999.

23 August 1947

When Roy Clarke played in the 4–3 win over Wolves on opening day, it meant that he had played three consecutive games in three different divisions. Clarke had played for Cardiff in Division Three in the penultimate game of the 1946/47 season before signing for City and featuring against Newport in the last match of City's Division Two title-winning campaign. His goal on debut then helped City get off to a winning start on their return to Division One.

23 August 1958

Two goals apiece from Joe Hayes and Bobby Johnstone overturned a three-goal deficit to win 4–3 against Burnley.

23 August 1986

Two goals from Graham Baker ensured Wimbledon's first ever game in the top flight, after rising from the non-league ranks, ended in defeat.

23 August 2000

It was a memorable home debut for Paulo Wanchope as he hit a hat-trick in City's rout of Sunderland, the Blues running out 4–2 winners.

23 August 2003

David Sommeil's goal earned a point for City as they hosted Portsmouth in the first ever league game at the City of Manchester Stadium.

24 August 1949

The trip to Fratton Park saw a second successive point to open the season as the Blues battled to a 1–1 draw.

24 August 1991

The 3–2 victory over Crystal Palace meant the Blues topped the table after three games when the first 'official' tables were published, having opened the season with a 100 per cent record.

24 August 1994

The 3–0 victory over West Ham saw the lowest crowd for a Premier League game at Maine Road. Just 19,150 saw the win due to the redevelopment of the Kippax Stand to turn Maine Road into an all-seater stadium.

25 August 1923

A crowd of 58,159 saw City beat Sheffield United 2–1 as the first ever game held at Maine Road signalled a new era for the club.

25 August 1948

City conceded a goal from Preston's Bobby Langton after just seven seconds of the new season. However, the Blues would hit back and go on to win the game 3–2.

25 August 1976

The 2–0 home victory over Aston Villa marked the first time the club had worn an all-blue kit. The club would later switch back to wearing white shorts for the 1985/86 season.

25 August 1990

Steve Redmond started on the bench on the opening day of the campaign at Tottenham after being an ever-present over the course of the previous three seasons.

26 August 1993

New General Manager John Maddock didn't take long to make his mark in the job as just a couple of games into the new season manager Peter Reid was sacked despite having guided the club to finishes of fifth, fifth and ninth during his time in charge. Although there had been some rumblings from the terraces over a perceived negative style of play, fans were overwhelmingly dismayed by the decision – especially considering Reid had been handed a new contract in the summer.

26 August 1996

After a tumultuous time in charge of the club, Alan Ball stepped down. A less than stellar managerial career continued into his time at City and after a horrific start to the season, not even a strong showing over the latter part could stave off a final-day relegation. Chairman Francis Lee was keen to show faith, but with fan unrest showing no sign of abating, Ball even suffered the ignominy of being booed by both sets of supporters as City fell to defeat at Stoke. Just three games into the season he resigned, leaving City hunting for yet another manager.

26 August 2000

After local-born Richard Edghill had become a target for the boo-boys, a horrific first-half performance against future City player Craig Bellamy resulted in Edghill being substituted in tears during the break. Edghill would be out of the side for a number of months, although he did later earn a recall to the side, ironically coming back into the line-up and turning in a stellar performance in the away fixture at Coventry.

26 August 2006

The club joined Stonewall's diversity scheme in a bid to become recognised as a gay-friendly employer. Chief Executive Alistair Mackintosh commented that 'we want to send a welcoming message to gay, lesbian and bisexual supporters, be inclusive and be a progressive employer.'

27 August 1960

With the scores level at 2–2, the game at Maine Road that season became the only Manchester derby to be abandoned as torrential rain caused the game to be halted early.

28 August 1937

The 3–1 defeat to Wolves on the opening day of the season ended a run of 22 games without a defeat.

28 August 1982

A 2–1 away win at Norwich was the first game that a City side sported a kit sponsor after car manufacturer Saab had agreed a deal to have its name across the front of their shirts.

28 August 1993

Fans didn't have to wait long for Peter Reid's successor but when it was announced that Brian Horton was the new man, many fans were decidedly underwhelmed, with Horton being christened 'Brian Who?'
Horton arrived at the club after managing in the lower leagues and was unfortunate in that he arrived as Peter Swales' grip on the club was slipping. He steered the club away from relegation in the first instance and introduced an attacking brand of football, but once Francis Lee assumed control his days were likely to be short-lived and Horton was sacked at the end of the 1994/95 season after a seventeenth-place finish.

29 August 1970

The club placed an announcement in *Shoot!* magazine to state that a new club badge would be worn in every game. Previously, the city coat of arms which was sported in Wembley cup finals was the only time a badge or crest was displayed.

29 August 1981

City's 2–1 victory over West Brom saw them earn
their first three points for a win under the new system
introduced that season, designed to encourage more
attacking football.

29 August 1998

The mixed start to life in the third tier of English football
continued as a Shaun Goater goal rescued a point away at
Notts County.

30 August 1887

A public meeting was held where it was announced that it
was the intention to form a new football club – Ardwick FC
– effectively being the day Manchester City was born.

30 August 1919

City drew 3–3 at home to Sheffield United in the first game
following the resumption of the league programme after
the end of the war.

30 August 1920

The Blues kicked off their season at home in style, beating Aston Villa 3–1. They would go unbeaten at home throughout the season but twelve defeats away from home cost them a chance of the title and they trailed in second place to champions Burnley.

31 August 1963

Derek Kevan kicked off a rich vein of scoring form as he grabbed both goals in the 2–1 victory away to Rotherham.

31 August 1994

City crashed to a 3–0 home defeat to Chelsea in the game that marked the club's centenary.

September

1 September 1894

The club were defeated 4–2 by Bury in their first game as 'Manchester City'.

1 September 1906

City's 4–1 defeat against Woolwich Arsenal was not just notable for being the first fixture played following the suspension of numerous players and officials following an FA investigation into the club's finances; with temperatures reportedly topping 90°F at kick off, the new-look City side were decimated as the club finished the game with just six men as a combination of dehydration and sunstroke meant that player after player was simply unable to continue in the game.

1 September 1942

Future City player Alan Oakes was born. Oakes was the cousin of another City great, Glyn Pardoe, and joined the club in 1958. During his time at City, Oakes would win a Division Two title, league title, FA Cup, European Cup Winners' Cup and two League Cups.

1 September 1993

Goals from Mike, Quinn and Vonk ensured new manager Brian Horton got off to a winning start as City boss with a 3–1 victory away to Swindon.

1 September 2008

Fans awoke to the news that under-siege Thaksin Shinawatra had elected to cut his losses and sell the club – little over a year after acquiring it – to ADUG, a group representing the interests of Sheikh Mansour, a member of the ruling Abu Dhabi royal family. Rumours of multi-million pound investments and transfer bids for the world's best players followed, and with the takeover coinciding with transfer deadline day, the club stunned fans by announcing the signing of Brazilian superstar Robinho, who was snatched from Real Madrid in an astonishing £32.5 million move.

2 September 1899

In their first ever fixture in the top flight City slipped to a 4–3 defeat to Blackburn.

2 September 1939

A 2–0 win over Chesterfield was the last league game of
the 1939/40 season due to the outbreak of war. During
the period where there was no league football, regional
wartime leagues were introduced and football continued,
albeit on a reduced basis.

2 September 2009

Following the arrival of big-money players Kolo Toure and
Joleon Lescott, club captain and four-time fans' player of
the year Richard Dunne was sold to Aston Villa after 296
appearances for the club. After the move was confirmed,
Dunne said, 'I'm delighted. It's a great opportunity for me.
Obviously Aston Villa have improved each season recently.
Hopefully I can be part of a squad that can challenge for a
Champions League spot.'

3 September 1892

In their first ever game as Ardwick, the club thrashed
Bootle by a 7–0 margin to go top of the table, a game
which also saw City miss a penalty.

3 September 1906

A trip to Goodison Park resulted in the club's biggest ever league defeat as they were hammered 9–1 by Everton.

3 September 1997

Midfielder Ged Brannan scored twice as Nottingham Forest were defeated 3–1 at the City Ground.

4 September 1920

Tommy Browell hit a hat-trick and took his tally to six in the first three games as the Blues edged out Liverpool 3–2.

4 September 1981

The club spent big, landing the classy striker Trevor Francis from Nottingham Forest for a fee of £1.3 million. Francis made an immediate impact, bagging two on debut in a 3–1 win at Stoke but suffered from a series of niggling injuries that restricted his effectiveness. Despite this he still managed 12 goals from 26 league starts. However, after just a solitary season at Maine Road Francis moved to Italian side Sampdoria.

4 September 1982

After losing Joe Corrigan through injury, Bobby McDonald
became the hero as he took over in goal and kept a clean
sheet that meant Dennis Tueart's goal was good enough to
beat Watford.

5 September 1927

Future manager on two separate occasions and overall
larger-than-life figure Malcolm Allison was born in Dartford.

5 September 1953

Don Revie and Johnny Hart struck to give City the win over
Manchester United in the first derby of the season.

5 September 1990

After jumping to challenge for an innocuous header in
the home game against Aston Villa, Paul Lake landed and
immediately collapsed to the floor. Although it didn't
appear to be too serious, Lake had damaged his cruciate
knee ligaments, an injury that would put him out of
football for almost two years.

6 September 1950

Blundell Park witnessed an eight-goal thriller as the goal-happy Blues and Grimsby played out a 4–4 draw.

6 September 1979

The club smashed the British transfer record to bring in Wolves midfielder Steve Daley. Daley would struggle to ever settle at Maine Road, with the side in the midst of much change under the stewardship of Malcolm Allison, and he could never recapture his Wolves form. With the fee weighing around his neck like a millstone, just twenty months later he was sold to the Seattle Sounders for a fee of £300,000 after only 4 goals in 48 appearances. It was a staggering loss of over £1 million on the player and subsequently, both Swales and then manager Malcolm Allison pointed an accusing finger at one another as to who was ultimately responsible for the decision to pay the inflated fee.

7 September 1921

The 1–1 draw at home to Liverpool ended a run of sixteen consecutive home wins.

7 September 1949

Frank Swift made his final appearance for the club and kept a clean sheet in a goalless draw at home to Everton.

8 September 1962

Goalkeeper Bert Trautmann was sent off for kicking the ball towards the referee after he conceded the Blues' fifth goal against West Ham. The Hammers went on to win the game 6–1.

9 September 1965

The home game against Norwich saw City level thanks to Neil Young's goal when the referee halted the game at half time due to a waterlogged pitch.

9 September 1992

David White's hot start to the league season saw him called up to the national squad and he made his England debut in a friendly against Spain. White saw an early opportunity saved and England fell to a 1–0 defeat, the game proving to be his one and only England cap.

9 September 2005

Former City player Mark Ward pleaded guilty to a charge of intent to supply four kilograms of cocaine and was sentenced to eight years in prison.

10 September 1974

Colin Bell hit a hat-trick as Scunthorpe were easily swept aside 6–0 in the second round of the League Cup.

11 September 1978

The club signed Polish international Kaziu Deyna for a fee of £100,000, and the Pole enjoyed moderate success at Maine Road, going on to score 13 goals in 39 games. The popular player sadly died in a car accident in 1989.

11 September 1993

Goals from Quinn, Flitcroft and Sheron saw the club stroll to a 3–0 home win over QPR as fan protests grew amid growing talk of an impending takeover by Francis Lee. The game was also the first at Maine Road for new manager Brian Horton.

12 September 1925

City and United played out a 1–1 draw in the first Manchester derby to be staged at Maine Road.

12 September 1970

Mike Doyle scored the only goal of the game as the Blues chalked up another win to remain unbeaten after seven games of the new season, defeating Nottingham Forest 1–0.

13 September 1913

A 3–1 win at Sheffield United ended a club record six consecutive draws, of which only one ended goalless.

13 September 1952

A 5–4 defeat to Middlesbrough was the first of ten games during the 1952/53 season that witnessed a total of six or more goals. The club would ultimately be relegated having scored 72 and conceded 87 over the course of the campaign.

13 September 1972

City contested their first ever UEFA Cup tie with a home fixture against Spanish outfit Valencia. Goals from Mellor and Marsh earned a creditable 2–2 draw.

13 September 2008

Robinho smashed home a free-kick just 15 minutes into his debut at home to Chelsea to add to the carnival atmosphere. City were the brighter side in the first half but Chelsea showed their quality after the break and ran out 3–1 winners.

14 September 1913

A 1–0 victory at home to Aston Villa signalled the official start of Ernest Mangnall's tenure in charge at the club.

14 September 2003

City's 4–1 victory over Aston Villa signalled the first victory at the new City of Manchester Stadium as well as the first penalty and hat-trick, both by Nicolas Anelka.

15 September 1962

After losing the previous four Manchester derbies, City came out on top at Old Trafford thanks to Joe Hayes winner that earned the Blues a 3–2 win.

15 September 1971

City drew 2–2 with Airdrieonians in their first ever appearance in the Texaco Cup, a competition set up for English, Scottish and Irish clubs who had not qualified for European competition. A below-strength side would go on to fall to a 2–0 defeat in the second leg in Scotland.

15 September 1976

Brian Kidd scored the only goal of the game as City defeated Juventus 1–0 in the first leg of their UEFA Cup first round tie.

16 September 1967

Stan Bowles scored the only two league goals of his City career during the Blues' 5–2 win over Sheffield United.

16 September 1995

Gerry Creaney scored a consolation goal in the 3–1 defeat away to Newcastle. Amid a forlorn start to the season it was the only goal the Blues managed in nine Premier League games.

17 September 1910

Watched by a crowd of around 60,000, City were defeated 2–1 by Manchester United in the first ever Manchester derby game to be staged at Old Trafford.

17 September 1949

A 4–2 defeat to Newcastle kick-started a wretched run of form that saw the Blues take just five points from ten games during their relegation season.

18 September 1965

Although beaten 3–2 by Cardiff City, the fixture at Ninian Park was notable for being the first game to see a City player introduced as a substitute get on the scoresheet. Matt Gray had been introduced for Johnny Crossan but his goal was not enough as the Blues fell to their first defeat of the season.

18 September 1968

Despite Malcolm Allison's comments that his league-winning side were set to 'terrorise Europe', the Blues disappointingly exited the European Cup at the very first stage to Fenerbahce as they were unable to overturn a 2–1 first leg deficit, being held to a scoreless draw in Turkey.

19 September 1925

Tommy Browell netted all four of City's goals in the 4–4 draw versus Everton which, although since matched on two further occasions, remains the highest scoring draw the club has contested.

19 September 1959

A pair from the prolific Joe Hayes earned bragging rights as City came on top against Manchester United by a 3–0 scoreline.

20 September 1947

The first post-war Manchester derby saw a goalless draw played out between the two sides, but is notable for having the largest attendance ever with a recorded crowd of 78,000 being present.

20 September 1986

Just seven games into the 1985/86 season, manager Billy McNeill stunned the club as he resigned to take charge of Aston Villa. The former Celtic manager had only been in charge for three seasons and had won promotion back to Division One following the 1984/85 campaign, but claimed 'influences in the background' were hampering his ability to effectively manage the club.

20 September 1997

During the 2–1 defeat at the hands of Norwich, Lee Bradbury finally got off the mark in a City shirt, scoring his first goal for the club in the seventh game of the season.

21 September 1968

The trio of Bell, Lee and Summerbee all got themselves on the scoresheet in the Blues' 4–0 victory at Roker Park against Sunderland.

21 September 2008

The 6–0 hammering of Portsmouth became the biggest
ever margin of victory in the short history of the City of
Manchester Stadium.

22 September 1962

A youthful Neil Young got himself on the scoresheet in
City's 2–2 draw at Blackpool.

22 September 1979

Michael Robinson hit two and Gary Owen scored the
other as City brushed Coventry aside to get back to
winning ways after suffering back-to-back defeats.

23 September 1970

Goals from Heslop and Lee saw City draw 2–2 against
Bologna in the second leg of their Anglo-Italian Cup clash
at Maine Road, a result that wasn't enough to see the Blues
through following their 1–0 defeat in the first leg three
weeks earlier.

23 September 1989

City came into the derby on the back of a 2–1 defeat to Brentford and were missing Andy Dibble, Neil McNab and £1 million striker Clive Allen from their side, while Manchester United featured recent big-money additions Danny Wallace, Paul Ince and Gary Pallister in their ranks. City, though, took a shock lead, with David Oldfield hitting home after Pallister had slipped in the box. Soon after Trevor Morley sent the crowd into raptures as he stabbed home following a scramble in the box. The goal prompted a pitch invasion as fans spilled onto the pitch from the North Stand and the two sides were led from the field. The delay didn't dampen City's momentum though, and they went further ahead as Ian Bishop's diving header sent the City fans delirious. Mark Hughes spectacularly reduced the arrears for Manchester United with a trademark bicycle kick to give United a lifeline, but any hopes they had of a comeback were thwarted as Paul Lake restored the advantage and Andy Hinchcliffe then powered a header firmly past a helpless Jim Leighton for the fifth and final goal to send Maine Road into ecstasy.

24 September 1932

Ernie Toseland scored two to help the Blues on the way to a fantastic 5–1 win over Blackpool.

24 September 1984

After over 100 appearances with the club, defender Kevin
Bond moved to Southampton.

25 September 1965

Stan Horne became the first black player to play for City in
the 1–0 victory over Derby. Signed from Aston Villa, Horne
played 50 games for the club between 1965 and 1968 and
in addition to setting a precedent at City, was also the first
black player at both Villa and Fulham.

25 September 1985

The 2–1 victory against Bury in the Milk Cup was played
not at Gigg Lane, but at Old Trafford as the Shakers
attempted to cash in on a potentially bigger crowd. They
would be disappointed, however, as a crowd of only
11,377 watched City take a slender lead into the
second leg.

26 September 1903

City maintained their 100 per cent start to the season with a comfortable 3–0 victory over Notts County.

26 September 1999

Not overly known for possessing stellar form on their travels, the 2–1 defeat at Ipswich did mark the end of City's fifteen-game unbeaten run – a large part of it earned during their surge up the Division Two table towards the end of the previous season.

26 September 2005

The club announced the launch of an advertising campaign that centred around proclaiming City as the 'real' team from Manchester. Denying it was an antagonistic move, the club stated that they merely wanted to 'emphasise the intrinsic bond between Manchester City Football Club and the city of Manchester.'

27 September 1972

City exited the first round of the UEFA Cup at the hands of Valencia as a 2–1 defeat on Spanish soil saw them exit 4–3 on aggregate.

27 September 1975

The 2–2 home derby that season was the first game at
Maine Road that saw fans on the Kippax segregated from
one another, a move that would soon become permanent.

27 September 1978

Goals from Brian Kidd and Colin Bell helped City
overcome FC Twente 3–2 to progress into the second
round of the UEFA Cup after the first leg had ended in a
1–1 draw.

28 September 1918

City hit seven past Bury in their Lancashire Section game
after regular League Cup games were put on hold as the
war continued and more players and officials began to
enlist.

28 September 1957

A fantastic 5–1 home win over Tottenham was even more
remarkable considering that in the previous week, the
Blues had suffered two crushing away defeats –
6–1 at Preston and 9–2 at West Brom. Unsurprisingly, it
was a season that saw plenty of goals at City, with the club

finishing the season having scored 104 and conceded 100 in their league campaign.

28 September 1974

Rodney Marsh's spectacular overhead kick that won the game against QPR was widely considered to be one of the best goals ever scored at Maine Road. QPR keeper Phil Parkes had kept the Blues at bay until 7 minutes from time when Marsh's opportunist strike won the points and left those in attendance marvelling over City's winner.

29 September 1956

City fell to a fourth successive defeat without scoring a goal as they were humbled 3–0 at Blackpool.

29 September 2007

Talented Brazilian Elano hit his first goal for the club with a spectacular long-range free-kick in the final minutes of the 3–1 victory at home to Newcastle.

30 September 1922

City drew 0–0 away to Huddersfield, a week after defeating
the Yorkshire side at home.

30 September 1989

During the 3–1 victory over Luton Town, veteran Paul
Cooper saved the fifty-sixth penalty of his career. The stopper
joined City in the twilight of his career from Ipswich but still
performed capably during his time at the club.

October

1 October 1971

Tony Towers, David Connor and Freddie Hill were all called into the squad for the weekend's trip to West Brom, but Neil Young was held back as he was still not deemed to be fit enough to return.

1 October 1981

Midfielder Asa Hartford was brought back to the club by manager John Bond, paying Everton a fee of £350,000 to reacquire the Scottish international who had been a victim of Malcolm Allison's purge at the end of the previous decade. Hartford remained at the club for a further three years before heading to America to try his hand in the NASL, having played 323 times for City. He would later return as part of the coaching set-up and had a couple of stints as caretaker manager in the mid-1990s.

2 October 1976

City bounced back from their first defeat of the season in the derby the previous week to beat West Ham 4–2, largely thanks to a brace from Dennis Tueart.

2 October 1995

The club floated on the specialist independent equity market OFEX exchange, being valued at £8 million in the process.

3 October 1987

With the inflatable craze continuing to sweep football, City players handed out inflatable bananas before the 4–2 win over Leicester at Maine Road.

4 October 1890

The club recorded their highest ever victory as they beat Liverpool Stanley 12–0 in the club's FA Cup qualifying round tie.

4 October 1924

Eric Roberts smashed his seventh goal in just three games as City went joint top of the table with Huddersfield and West Brom following a 3–1 win against West Ham.

4 October 1971

Rumours surfaced in the press that the club hierarchy were considering the possibility of reconstructing the current managerial set up which could leave Joe Mercer marginalised as a result.

4 October 1995

During the 4–0 win over Wycombe in the second leg of the club's Littlewoods Cup tie, Richard Edghill went down injured with City having already used two substitutes. With just one substitute remaining only reserve goalkeeper Martyn Margetson was available to be called upon. The Welshman was then introduced in an attacking role and actually came close to getting his name on the scoresheet but couldn't quite convert a decent opportunity that came his way late on.

5 October 1957

The 4–0 defeat away to Birmingham marked the only game in which the Blues failed to score in the season where they both scored and conceded over 100 goals.

5 October 1968

The 2–0 defeat away to Everton was the first time that the club had sported the iconic red and black striped away kit.

5 October 1971

It was announced that Mike Summerbee had been recalled to the England squad for the important Euro '72 Group game against Switzerland.

5 October 1972

Club director Peter Swales replaced Eric Alexander as chairman of Manchester City. Alexander had succeeded his father, Albert, as chairman but stepped down as he felt he did not have sufficient time to devote to the club. Swales was an ambitious figure who had made his fortune in the TV and radio rentals business and had great plans for the club to become the premier footballing side in Manchester.

6 October 1956

Low on confidence after four successive defeats, the Blues crashed once again as they were outplayed at Arsenal and ended up on the wrong end of a 7–3 scoreline.

7 October 1949

The club signed goalkeeper Bert Trautmann. Replacing the legendary Frank Swift was never going to be an easy task, but for Bremen-born Trautmann, the weight of history ensured it was an even harder one. He had been a German paratrooper and prisoner-of-war but at the end of the war opted to refuse an offer of repatriation. The signing of Trautmann caused initial protest from a number of groups who were unhappy that a German had been signed so soon after the end of the war and over 20,000 demonstrated at the decision to sign him. Trautmann's performances and demeanour meant he would win over the doubters and he went on to make 545 appearances for City. In 2004 he was awarded an honorary OBE for his work in developing Anglo-German relations through football with his Trautmann Foundation.

7 October 1950

Unbeaten in ten games, a Smith hat-trick gave a confident City side a 3–0 lead over Doncaster by half time. However, it would prove to be a totally different City side in the second half as the Blues collapsed and conceded four unanswered goals as Rovers ran out 4–3 winners.

7 October 1971

After a gradual decline in their relationship, brought about by a boardroom battle that placed them in different camps added to Malcolm Allison's desire for greater control, Allison took the position of team manager with Joe Mercer 'moving upstairs' to became General Manager. It was the beginning of a sad end to a successful union between the pair and resulted in Mercer's eventual move to become manager at Coventry City.

7 October 1996

Following the departure of Alan Ball, Asa Hartford had performed the role of caretaker manager for a six-week period while the board searched for Ball's successor. That man was announced as Steve Coppell, the manager who had built a good reputation in charge of Crystal Palace. Coppell was a former Manchester United player which didn't endear him to some, but brought with him the much-needed traits of stability and longevity.

8 October 1980

The club hoped the return of Malcolm Allison would be the final push to success but the 1980/81 season had begun badly with the club at the wrong end of the table. In addition, Allison had spent big on the likes of Steve Daley, while favourites such as Brian Kidd, Dave Watson, Gary Owen, Peter Barnes and Asa Hartford had all been sold. Intriguingly, Allison's last days were played out in front of a TV crew who were filming a documentary on City. A 1–0 defeat to Leeds was to be the final straw and Allison was dismissed. Chairman Peter Swales would later insist that the decision to bring back Allison was his worst mistake.

8 October 1988

Bill Williams made his one and only appearance for the club as a substitute in a 1–0 defeat at Ipswich. Signed from Stockport for a £50,000 fee, he was transferred back less than two months later.

9 October 1967

Twenty-three-year-old Francis Lee was signed from Bolton for £60,000. Although small in height, Lee was a strong player and difficult to knock off the ball. His arrival went a long way in helping the club win the league title that season as he scored 16 goals in just 31 games. Lee won a number of honours in addition to becoming an England regular during his time at the club and many felt that he was sold prematurely when he moved to Derby in 1974.

9 October 1971

Francis Lee's goal helped Malcolm Allison get off to a successful start in his first game in sole charge of the club as Everton were beaten 1–0.

10 October 1903

The 1–0 defeat at St James' Park at the hands of Newcastle ended a run of six consecutive away victories, a record that stands to this day.

10 October 1959

A McAdams hat-trick saw City hammer Preston 5–1 on the road, their fourth consecutive win following a somewhat patchy start to the season.

10 October 1960

The 1–1 draw against Tottenham ended the North Londoners' eleven-match winning streak.

11 October 1986

Along with results elsewhere, the 3–1 defeat against
Newcastle saw City drop to the bottom of the table with
just seven points from the first ten games of the season.

12 October 1988

The second leg of the Littlewoods Cup second round tie at
Home Park against Plymouth was finally played after being
postponed a day earlier. After leading 1–0 from the first
leg, two goals from Nigel Gleghorn helped the Blues to a
convincing 6–3 win. The two teams also met in the league
just seventy-two hours later at the same venue, with many
City fans deciding to stay down in Devon for a couple of
extra days. The Blues again came out on top, this time with
a narrower margin of victory as Brian Gayle's strike was
enough to make it a successful week on the south coast.

13 October 1951

A 1–0 win at home to Preston was the second in successive
weeks and saw the club ease away from the bottom three.

14 October 1953

A friendly against Scottish side Hearts marked the first time that the floodlights were used at Maine Road, with City running out 6–3 winners.

14 October 1985

A hat-trick from Gordon Davies gave the Blues a comprehensive 6–1 victory over Leeds in the Full Members' Cup. The big win was, however, watched by just 4,029 hardy souls at Maine Road.

14 October 1989

For their away fixture at Arsenal, City sported a new yellow away kit for the first time. It didn't change the club's poor run of form against the Gunners as they crashed to a 3–0 defeat and the kit was never worn again.

15 October 1983

The Blues slipped to a 1–0 defeat at Charlton, their first defeat in eight games after starting the season brightly under new boss Billy McNeill.

15 October 1994

City held on for victory at QPR to win 2–1, ending up with just nine men in the process. Comfortably leading 2–0 through Flitcroft and Walsh, the Blues saw Andy Dibble sent off for a professional foul, followed shortly after by Richard Edghill for two bookable offences. Substitute goalkeeper Tony Coton, on the bench as he was returning to full fitness, stood firm in the face of a late onslaught to secure the points.

16 October 2004

City were the only side to beat Chelsea during their title-winning season as an early penalty from Nicolas Anelka earned the Blues a 1–0 win.

17 October 1964

Despite Derek Kevan hitting his tenth goal of the campaign, the Blues fell to a 3–2 defeat against managerless Huddersfield.

17 October 1980

After thrashing out a compensation package with Norwich City, the Blues appointed John Bond as the replacement for the sacked Malcolm Allison. With City at the wrong end of the table, Bond brought in a series of veterans such Gerry Gow and Tommy Hutchison and a climb away from the relegation zone was matched by an FA Cup run that took the Blues all the way to a Wembley final. The following season began promisingly with the addition of Trevor Francis, but the club's finances prevented Bond from really pushing on. Bond would eventually leave the club in February 1983 after an FA Cup defeat to lower-league Brighton.

17 October 1987

City fell to a listless 3–0 defeat away to Ipswich, a performance that saw manager Mel Machin play several of the side in the following midweek reserve game.

18 October 1951

Don Revie was signed from Hull City for £25,000. Revie would go on to be known more for his managerial exploits in charge of Leeds and England, but was an important part of a City side in the early part of the 1950s. Although he struggled during his first couple of seasons, Revie was deployed in a new role as a deep-lying centre forward, which became known as the 'Revie Plan'. The 1954/55 season saw City reach the FA Cup final and Revie became the first City player to be voted as the Football Writers' Player of the Year in 1955. Revie, however, fell out with manager Leslie McDowall the following season and although recalled for the FA Cup final win in 1956, moved on to Sunderland later that year.

18 October 1978

City set themselves up well in their UEFA Cup tie against Standard Liège as two goals from Brian Kidd saw them victorious by a 4–0 margin in the first leg.

18 October 2003

The second half of the fixture against Bolton exploded into life. At 1–1 at half time the game looked tight, but City romped home after the break and ran out comfortable 6–2 winners despite seeing Shaun Wright-Phillips sent off.

19 October 1957

City comfortably defeated Blackpool 5–2 with in-form strike duo Barlow and Hayes both getting on the scoresheet.

20 October 1906

Two goals from Irvine Thornley gave City a 4–2 victory
against Aston Villa in the first meeting of the clubs since
the FA's decision to suspend a number of City players and
officials as a result of the allegations stemming from the
clubs' clash at the end of the 1904/05 season.

21 October 1972

City hoisted themselves out of the relegation zone as two
goals from Rodney Marsh earned a much-needed 4–3 win
over West Ham at Maine Road. The club's poor start to the
season hard largely been as a result of seven successive
away defeats and it would take until mid-February before
the first win on their travels was achieved.

21 October 1987

In their seventh away fixture of the season, City's 4–2 win
at Bradford City ended a run of thirty-four games away
from home without a win. The relegation the Blues had
suffered the previous campaign had largely been as a result
of them going winless away from home throughout the
whole season.

21 October 1995

The 0–0 home draw against Leeds brought to an end a run of eight consecutive defeats that the club suffered at the start of Alan Ball's time in charge at the club.

22 October 1923

Future City hero Bert Trautmann was born in Bremen, Germany.

22 October 1973

Johnny Hart's brief tenure as City manager came to an end as he stepped down following a period of ill-health. Despite being a member of the backroom staff at the club after retiring as a player, Hart had been a surprise choice six months earlier as the man to replace Malcolm Allison and would later admit that he never felt comfortable being in charge.

22 October 1980

The 3–1 win over Tottenham signalled the first league win of the season after twelve games without a win.

22 October 1994

The club's wild 5–2 win over Tottenham at Maine Road was almost certainly the game of the decade. Although struggling under manager Brian Horton, he had assembled a side full of attacking intent and, in Nicky Summerbee and Peter Beagrie, he had two old-fashioned wingers. Their opponents that day were equally attacking under Ossie Ardiles and the game was a classic. After falling behind early, City stormed to a 3–1 lead at half time with two goals from Paul Walsh and a Niall Quinn strike. City allowed their opponents back into the game just a minute into the second half but the inspirational Walsh set up Steve Lomas and then Garry Flitcroft to cap a fine 5–2 victory, a game many fans of a certain age consider to be their favourite ever City game.

23 October 2005

City fan Helen Turner, best known for her bell-ringing in the North Stand during games, passed away after a long life, much of which was spent following City around the country.

24 October 1925

Five goals from Tommy Browell saw the Blues beat Burnley
8–3 at Maine Road. Just two days later, City were defeated
by the same scoreline against Sheffield United.

25 October 1977

Peter Barnes' goal gave City a second bite at the cherry in
their third round League Cup tie at Luton. It took a second
replay but the Blues ultimately edged out the lower-
league side.

26 October 1986

Mick McCarthy's towering header earned a point in the
1–1 draw at home to United in the first ever live televised
Manchester derby.

26 October 1988

City slipped to a disappointing 1–0 midweek defeat away
to West Brom. After being largely blamed for the goal after

a misjudging a hopefully-hit long ball, in his post-match interview captain Brian Gayle would blame the floodlights at The Hawthorns, claiming that he lost the flight of the ball in the bright night lights.

27 October 1987

Two goals from Imre Varadi and one from Paul Stewart gave the Blues a 3–0 win over Nottingham Forest in the third round of the Littlewoods Cup, a huge surprise given the success that Forest enjoyed in the competition in the mid- to late 1980s.

27 October 1990

Two goals from David White and a strike from Colin Hendry had put City on the verge of a second successive derby win at Maine Road, but after withdrawing midfield general Peter Reid late in the game, Howard Kendall saw his side surrender a 3–1 lead as Manchester United stormed back to snatch a late point.

28 October 1981

After their Milk Cup second round clash against Stoke finished 2–0 on aggregate after extra time, Joe Corrigan saved the twentieth spot kick of the shoot-out to see City win 9–8 on penalties.

28 October 1995

City's woeful start to the season reached its nadir with a 6–0 defeat at Anfield against Liverpool that capped a miserable week, given that it came just three days after the Blues had exited the Coca-Cola Cup at the same venue 4–0.

29 October 1998

With the Blues struggling to adjust to life in Division Two, Joe Royle made a splash in the transfer market by signing out-of-favour Huddersfield centre-half Andy Morrison. Morrison had bounced round a number of clubs in his career but Royle saw his determination and leadership abilities as being vital to helping steer the club back on track. Installed as club captain, Morrison's influence was vital in the Blues' promotion at the first attempt that season.

30 October 1967

Future City player David White was born in Urmston. White progressed through the youth ranks to make his debut in the mid-1980s alongside the likes of Steve Redmond, Paul Lake, Ian Brightwell and Andy Hinchcliffe, forming the nucleus of a new-look Blues side. A fast-paced winger, White also played at times in attack and scored 96 goals in 341 games for the club before moving to Leeds in a swap deal for David Rocastle.

30 October 1971

Colin Bell made his 100th appearance for the club in the 1–1 draw against Huddersfield.

31 October 1953

City edged out Burnley in a narrow 3–2 win at Maine Road in front of a crowd of 32,353.

November

1 November 1972

Future City player Paul Dickov was born. The forward's all-action and energetic style was described by manager Joe Royle as being 'like a dog chasing waste paper'. The Scottish international had two spells at the club, scoring 41 times in 181 appearances, including the goal at Wembley that was voted as City's greatest ever.

1 November 2004

Irishman Willo Flood scored the only league goal of his City career in the 1–1 draw against Norwich.

2 November 1946

Andy Black grabbed a hat-trick as the Blues put five past West Brom without reply.

2 November 1988

Former youth team star Paul Moulden netted a hat-trick as the Blues progressed to round four of the Littlewoods Cup with a 4–2 victory against Sheffield United.

2 November 1991

The 3–0 victory over Southampton – featuring goals from both Mike Sheron and Niall Quinn – was the fourth in succession and saw the Blues move up to third in the table and just three points off leaders Manchester United.

3 November 1894

The first league meeting between Manchester City and Newton Heath ended with the Blues being defeated 5–2, despite a brace of goals from Billy Meredith.

3 November 1937

City defeated Sunderland 2–0 in the Charity Shield game that was staged at Maine Road before the annual showpiece fixture was moved to Wembley.

4 November 1970

After heavy rain fell during City's 2–0 second leg win over Honvéd in round two of the European Cup Winners' Cup, captain Tony Book revealed how concerned he had been that the game may have been called off at half time, saying, 'I'd been scared right from the start that the referee might call the game off. The rain was getting heavier and I knew that if he intended to stop it would be during the interval.'

4 November 1995

Nicky Summerbee scored to give the Blues their first league victory of the season by beating Bolton 1–0. After opening their campaign without a win in twelve games, the victory would see City post a five-game unbeaten run.

5 November 1990

Howard Kendall stunned City by walking out of the club to return to previous side Everton, calling them a 'marriage' while City were merely an 'affair'. Kendall was unable to restore former glories to Goodison Park, while the man who replaced him – Peter Reid – guided the Blues to a pair of fifth-place finishes.

6 November 1920

Fire destroyed the main stand at Hyde Road. As well as the structural damage caused by the blaze, many of the club's records and archives from their early history were also destroyed.

6 November 1971

One of the greatest derby games of all time ended in a thrilling 3–3 draw. City trailed both 2–0 and 3–2 in the game but a late strike from Mike Summerbee rescued a point for the Blues at the death.

7 November 1987

Tony Adcock, Paul Stewart and David White all hit hat-tricks as City romped to a 10–1 win over Huddersfield. The Blues had struggled early on in the game but after Neil McNab opened the scoring they jumped out to a 4–0 lead at the half-time mark. City were utterly dominant in the second half, however, and the goals rained in as David White completed his hat-trick to make it 9–0 with 5 minutes remaining. Huddersfield – to cheers from the whole of Maine Road – pulled a goal back from former Blue Andy May's penalty, but with the crowd demanding a tenth goal, David White slid home in the final minute to send Maine Road into delirium.

7 November 1992

City defeated Leeds 4–0 at Maine Road for the second season in succession, with both victories coming inside the same calendar year.

8 November 1919

A Tommy Browell hat-trick saw City coast to an 8–2 victory over Blackburn.

8 November 1996

Just six games into his City career, Steve Coppell resigned as manager from the club on medical grounds, citing the pressures involved with the job, bringing about the end of what is the shortest spell in charge of any City manager.

8 November 2006

In his column in the *Manchester Evening News*, Chris Bailey called on the club to investigate the possibility of selling the naming rights to the City of Manchester Stadium, writing, 'It is hard to envisage any City fan being up in arms at the thought of their new home receiving a fresh name. Even those Blues who perpetually view life through a half-empty glass must see that it could benefit them and the team by providing a cash injection to a club always seeking ways of producing worthwhile investment.'

9 November 1974

The 1–0 win against Stoke City marked Alan Oakes' 500th game for the club.

9 November 2002

Maine Road's final season witnessed a famous Manchester derby win as two goals from Shaun Goater and a further strike from Nicolas Anelka gave the Blues a 3–1 win over an outplayed United side.

10 November 1987

After going goal crazy against Huddersfield three days earlier, the Blues once again went on the rampage as they defeated Plymouth 6–2. On-fire Tony Adcock – one of the hat-trick heroes during the 10–1 win, helped himself to another hat-trick.

10 November 1994

With on-loan goalkeeper Simon Tracey in goal, City slumped to their worst ever Manchester derby defeat as they suffered a demoralising 5–0 loss at Old Trafford to a rampant Manchester United side.

10 November 1956

After a fall-out that sidelined him for the majority of the preceeding season, Don Revie left the club to join Sunderland for a fee of £24,000.

11 November 1924

The departure of Horace Barnes to Preston North End brought to an end Barnes' incredible scoring run at the club. During his ten years at City, Barnes scored 198 goals in just 308 games, striking up a terrific partnership with Tommy Browell. He was also the first ever player to score at Maine Road.

11 November 1990

During the 3–2 defeat to Leeds United, a banner in the North Stand read 'Kendall robbed Mavis and Derek' – a reference to a recent *Coronation Street* storyline and aimed at Howard Kendall who had that week walked out on the club to rejoin Everton.

12 November 1881

The first ever derby between the modern-day Manchester City and Manchester United took place as St Mark's took on Newton Heath, with Newton Heath running out 3–0 winners.

12 November 1975

Despite a 4–0 win over Manchester United in the fourth round of the League Cup, the game saw a serious injury suffered by Colin Bell during a challenge with United's Martin Buchan. Although Bell did make a return to the side, the injury he suffered effectively curtailed his career at just twenty-nine years of age.

13 November 1880

The club's first game as St Mark's Gorton, against a Baptist Church side from Macclesfield, ended in a 2–1 defeat.

13 November 1996

Reeling from Steve Coppell's resignation, the Blues slumped to a 3–2 home defeat to Oxford despite Phil Neal's pre-game salute to the Kippax.

14 November 1914

The Blues had opened the season with an impressive eleven-game unbeaten run but came unstuck against The Wednesday as they fell to a 2–1 defeat. The league that season saw just six points separate positions 1 and 11. Despite their strong start, the club failed to win any of their last five games and lost their last three to finish in fifth position and just three points off Champions Everton.

14 November 1959

Alan Oakes made his debut in a 1–1 draw against Chelsea. As well as making the most total appearances for the club, Oakes also holds the record number of league appearances with 564.

15 November 1968

Uwe Rösler was born in the East German town of
Altenburg. Rösler signed for the club from Dynamo
Dresden as a relative unknown in March 1994 but very
quickly established himself as a cult hero. Rösler would
play a vital role in helping the Blues avoid relegation in
his first couple of seasons but after the club dropped into
Division Two he moved to Bundesliga side Kaiserslautern.

15 November 1990

After a spell as caretaker manager following the departure
of Howard Kendall, Peter Reid was given the job on a
permanent basis after receiving the backing of the majority
of the supporters.

16 November 1949

Maine Road hosted a home international that saw England
comfortably defeat Northern Ireland by a 9–2 scoreline.

17 November 1979

A rare bright spot in the City career of Steve Daley saw him grab the winner in the victory over Bolton.

17 November 2005

The *Manchester Evening News* reported that Stuart Pearce was set to be handed a transfer kitty 'in the region of £10 million' to strengthen his squad.

18 November 1948

Future City and England goalkeeper Joe Corrigan was born in Manchester.

18 November 1995

Martin 'Buster' Phillips was signed for £500,000 from Exeter with manager Alan Ball stating that Phillips would eventually become football's first £10 million player. Three years later and having made just fifteen appearances, the winger was sold to Portsmouth for a knockdown fee of £100,000.

19 November 1938

Peter Doherty's brace was good enough to help the Blues to a 3–0 victory at home to Coventry City.

19 November 1949

The 3–0 defeat at Burnden Park to Bolton was the Blues' third successive defeat and saw them slip into the bottom three.

20 November 1976

Dennis Tueart hit the only goal of the game as the Blues took the points following a 1–0 win against West Brom.

20 November 2009

Craig Bellamy expressed concern over his long-term future as a history of knee problems cast a shadow over his fitness, saying, 'I know there are not four or five years ahead of me, not with the injuries I've had. Maybe I've got one or two years at the most. It will be all over before I know it, so I'm just enjoying it.'

21 November 1960

City's 2–0 defeat at Fratton Park against Portsmouth was the club's first ever defeat in the League Cup, a competition that the Blues would go on to enjoy huge success in over the next decade or so.

21 November 1970

Francis Lee hit both goals in City's 2–0 victory over West Ham.

22 November 1980

The good run of form under new manager John Bond continued as the Blues brushed aside Coventry 3–0 with goals from Dave Bennett, Paul Power and Kevin Reeves.

22 November 2003

The 3–0 defeat to Newcastle would be Eyal Berkovic's last game in a City shirt. The talented playmaker had made a bright start at the club and struck up an effective partnership with Ali Benarbia, but fell out with Kevin Keegan and was sold to Portsmouth.

23 November 1961

Steve Mackenzie was born. The Romford-born midfielder moved to City in 1979 for a fee of £250,000 – a record fee for a teenager at the time and even more remarkable considering he had yet to play a first team game for Crystal Palace. Although he only enjoyed a brief career at the club before moving to West Brom, Mackenzie's goal in the 1981 FA Cup final replay would go down as one of the best ever cup final goals.

23 November 1978

Finally getting the game underway after the previous day's postponement, City earned a credible 2–2 draw with Milan at the San Siro to leave the second leg of their UEFA Cup clash perfectly poised.

23 November 2003

Joey Barton missed out on a chance of a City debut as he had misplaced his shirt when called upon by manager Kevin Keegan during the Premier League game away to Middlesbrough.

24 November 1956

The Blues continued their recent renaissance with a 5–1 thumping of Portsmouth. It capped an unbeaten spell that saw them rise from twenty-first to fifteenth in the table.

24 November 1973

Following the resignation of Malcolm Allison, Peter Swales made Norwich City manager Ron Saunders the first of his eleven managerial appointments. Swales heralded the appointment and believed Saunders' tough reputation would work wonders at the club. Amid reports of player unrest, Saunders lasted only five months – brief even by Swales' reputation.

25 November 1946

City terrace hero Mike Doyle was born. Doyle, a determined figure on the pitch was always likely to endear himself to fans but his loathing of Manchester United gave him a special place in fans' hearts. Perhaps never quite given the credit he deserved as a player, Doyle also captained the side in the 1976 League Cup final before moving to Stoke in the summer of 1978.

25 November 1995

Bert Trautmann opened the new all-seater Kippax Stand prior to the game against Aston Villa. Gio Kinkladze would go on to score the only goal in the Blues' 1–0 win.

26 November 1949

Bert Trautmann made his home debut in the 4–0 win over Birmingham, sparking an increase in attendances which had dropped off in the weeks prior to him pulling on a City jersey.

26 November 1969

The 5–0 second leg win over SK Lierse in the European Cup Winners' Cup second round tie saw the Blues progress with an 8–0 aggregate win; the highest winning margin in the club's history in European competition.

26 November 1989

Just months after guiding the Blues to a famous 5–1 victory over Manchester United, manager Mel Machin was sacked by Peter Swales, with the City chairman stating Machin was simply 'not charismatic enough' and was concerned with his inability to connect with the fans. Machin spent two-and-a-half years in charge and guided the side to promotion in 1988/89, with many of the younger players who formed the core of the City side that achieved high league finishes in the early 1990s.

27 November 1907

Eric Brook, City's most prolific goalscorer, was born. Brook joined the club in 1928 along with Fred Tilson from Barnsley for combined £6,000 and hit 158 goals in 450 appearances before retiring after the 1939/40 season. Brook also scored ten 10 goals in 18 international games for England.

27 November 1993

The 3–1 home loss to Sheffield Wednesday saw Niall Quinn suffer a cruciate knee ligament injury that ruled him out for the remainder of the season and caused him to miss the 1994 World Cup.

27 November 2003

City paid the price for not taking a lead from their first leg tie as a lifeless 0–0 draw at Polish side Groclin saw them exit the UEFA Cup that season at the second round stage.

28 November 1934

The Blues crashed to a 4–0 defeat against Arsenal in the Charity Shield.

28 November 1970

Title-chasing Leeds ensured City had another disappointing away day as they fell to a 1–0 defeat at Elland Road.

29 November 1993

Following an intense and populist wave of support, Peter Swales finally ceded control of the club to the consortium headed by Francis Lee and stepped down after almost twenty turbulent years at the helm of the club.

29 November 1995

After a desperate start to the season, an unbeaten run in November saw manager Alan Ball named as the Premier League manager of the month.

30 November 1985

Despite Mark Lillis' third goal in four games, a visit to Luton saw the Blues on the wrong end of a 2–1 scoreline.

30 November 2002

Goals from Steve Howey and Eyal Berkovic earned a 2–0 win over Bolton at Maine Road.

December

1 December 1906

City defeated Manchester United 3–0 at Hyde Road in the first top-flight derby. The backdrop to the game was perhaps more noteworthy. Negotiations were conducted following the game that led to the transfer to Manchester United of many of the players who had been banned as a result of the FA investigation into the club earlier in the year.

1 December 1996

Wolves did the double over the Blues during 1995/96 after an emphatic 3–0 victory at Molineux.

2 December 1939

Jimmy Heale netted five of the six City goals in their high-scoring 6–6 encounter with Stockport County in a game played in the Western Division section of the Wartime

Regional League. The Football League season had been abandoned in early September of that year following the outbreak of the Second World War.

2 December 1946

The City hierarchy made a popular decision by appointing former captain Sam Cowan to replace the long-serving Wilf Wild as manager at the club.

3 December 1921

The club's 42-game unbeaten home record was brought to an end as the Blues fell to a 3–2 defeat against Bolton. During the unbeaten stretch, the club posted an impressive 33 victories.

3 December 1969

Goals from Bell and Lee gave City a slender 2–1 advantage over Manchester United to set up a mouthwatering second leg of the League Cup semi-final at Old Trafford.

3 December 1996

It was revealed that Stephen Boler was the third man involved in the JD Sports consortium looking to take control of the club and that their overall investment would realise around £11 million.

4 December 1993

Mike Sheron's sixth goal of the season against Leeds was in vain as the Blues fell to a 3–2 defeat, but it was his last goal for the club before he joined Norwich City the following March. In a season where City struggled for goals, Sheron would remarkably finish the season as the club's top goalscorer.

4 December 2005

The 5–2 victory over Charlton signalled the beginning of a month of contrasting goalscoring fortunes. In the six games the Blues contested during the month, they netted twelve times but failed to hit the net in three of the games that were played.

5 December 1908

An Irvine Thornley hat-trick helped the Blues hit Bury for six in the 6–1 defeat of the Shakers.

5 December 1987

Goalkeeper Eric Nixon saw red after lashing out at Crystal Palace forward Ian Wright during the 3–1 defeat at Maine Road.

6 December 1978

A memorable European night at Maine Road saw City turn in a famous performance as – after a 2–2 draw at the San Siro in the first leg – goals from Booth, Hartford and Kidd by half time helped the Blues to a 3–0 victory over the Italians.

6 December 1999

BSkyB acquired a 9.95 per cent stake in the club for £5.5 million.

7 December 1957

A hat-trick of penalties from Ken Barnes helped the Blues to an emphatic 6–2 victory over Everton at Maine Road.

7 December 1968

In an otherwise disappointing defence of their league title, the Blues had a rare bright spot as they thrashed Burnley 7–0.

8 December 1989

After Mel Machin was sacked, Peter Swales turned to Howard Kendall after Oldham manager Joe Royle had rejected the opportunity to take over at Maine Road. Kendall had led Everton to much success in the mid-1980s and his appointment was seen as the type of big name that City needed. Kendall overhauled much of the squad over the course of the season and made the Blues much harder to beat, losing just five of his thirty-two league games in charge.

8 December 1998

Just 3,007 fans were in attendance to watch City's Auto Windscreens Shield tie against Mansfield. The competition was for clubs in the bottom two divisions in the Football League and with City's focus on escaping the third tier at the first attempt, Joe Royle fielded a largely second-string side. The Blues fell to a 2–1 defeat in front of the lowest ever crowd for a game at Maine Road.

9 December 1967

One of the most famous games at Maine Road occurred
during the league-winning season in 1967/68. The Blues
stormed to a 4–1 victory over Tottenham in icy conditions,
leading to the match being dubbed as the 'Ballet on
Ice' owing to the way in which the Blues dealt with the
elements in comparison to the visitors. Goals from Bell,
Coleman, Summerbee and Young secured the victory that
led to Jimmy Greaves to laud, 'the way the City lads had
moved so gracefully in those conditions, while we were
falling about like clowns at the circus.'

10 December 1988

Doubles from Ian Brightwell and Paul Moulden in a 4–0
victory over Bradford City sent the Blues to top of
the league.

10 December 2009

After battling back from a long-term injury, it was reported
that midfielder Michael Johnson had been ruled out for the
season after suffering a knee injury during training.

11 December 1962

The 6–0 reversal suffered at the hands of Birmingham City was the club's biggest ever League Cup defeat.

11 December 1971

Manager Malcolm Allison was named as manager of the month for November after an unbeaten spell that yielded three wins and a draw.

11 December 1985

Goals from David Phillips and Jim Melrose saw off Hull as a 2–0 victory overturned a first leg defeat and sent the Blues to Wembley to face Chelsea in the Full Members' Cup final.

12 December 1924

Sam Cowan was signed from Doncaster Rovers. An inspirational figure, Cowan spent over a decade at the club as a player, making 407 appearances and he became the only City player to play in three separate FA Cup finals.

12 December 1970

Francis Lee's hat-trick saw the Blues to an impressive 4–1 win over Manchester United at Old Trafford, but the victory was overshadowed by the broken leg suffered by Glyn Pardoe in a tackle with George Best. So severe was the injury that surgeons at one point feared the leg might have to be amputated.

13 December 1952

Roy Clarke and Johnny Hart were both on the scoresheet in the impressive 4–0 win over Chelsea.

13 December 1997

Georgian defender Murtaz Shelia was on target on his debut during the 2–1 defeat to Birmingham.

14 December 1929

Tommy Johnson netted to help the Blues to a narrow 3–2 win over Leicester.

14 December 1985

Two goals apiece from Gordon Davies and Paul Simpson
helped the Blues to their most emphatic victory of the
season – a 5–1 win against Coventry.

15 December 1956

City's 3–2 defeat at home to Wolves was the first ever
televised game at Maine Road, with the BBC carrying
match highlights. The match also saw the return of Bert
Trautmann to the side in what was his first game back
following his FA Cup final injury at the end of the previous
season.

15 December 1984

Jim Melrose scored for the third game in succession as the
Blues defeated Charlton 3–1.

15 December 1990

In the 2–1 home win over Tottenham, City had to wear the
away kit due to foggy conditions meaning the blue home
shirts were too similar to Tottenham's white shirts. The
maroon kit proved a winner, though, as goals from Mark
Ward and Steve Redmond earned the points.

16 December 1967

Francis Lee struck to earn a rare point at Anfield as the two
sides battled out a 1–1 draw.

17 December 1960

City slumped to their seventh defeat in a row as they fell
2–1 to Nottingham Forest.

17 December 1969

The Blues' 2–2 draw at Old Trafford against Manchester
United secured a 4–3 aggregate win and sent City through
to Wembley for the first of three League Cup finals in just
six seasons.

18 December 1965

Mike Doyle scored twice as the Blues rounded off the year
well with a 2–0 defeat of Crystal Palace that left them well
placed in the Division Two promotion positions.

18 December 1982

Kevin Bond hit his first goal of the season in the 1–1 draw with Brighton.

19 December 1994

German midfielder Maurizio Gaudino was signed on a loan deal from Eintracht Frankfurt. Although he only had a brief spell at Maine Road, Gaudino would prove to be a popular figure with fans thanks to his stylish play.

19 December 2009

The 4–3 victory over Sunderland was played against the backdrop of growing rumours and uncertainty over Mark Hughes' future. Just hours after the final whistle, Hughes was axed having only had eighteen months in charge of the club, and replaced by former Inter Milan manager Roberto Mancini.

20 December 1924

Sam Cowan – who went on to have both a distinguished playing career and brief spell in charge of the club

– made his debut for City in the 2–2 draw against
Birmingham City.

21 December 1901

City's game against Stoke was abandoned after 70 minutes
with Stoke leading 2–0. It was the only game out of the
nineteen City have had abandoned that they were behind
at the point it was called off.

21 December 1991

A late goal from David White – his second of the game –
rescued a point at Anfield in the 2–2 draw with Liverpool.

22 December 1990

Peter Reid suffered his first defeat in charge of the club as
future City manager Steve Coppell's Crystal Palace side
defeated the Blues 2–0.

22 December 1993

Long-time Blue David White's City career was brought
to an end as the pacy forward moved to Leeds in a swap

for midfielder David Rocastle. White was just short of a
century of goals, scoring 96 times before heading to
Elland Road.

23 December 1933

After three successive victories, City headed to Molineux
to take on Wolves, but a desperate display saw the side
suffer one of the heaviest losses in the club's history as they
slumped to an 8–0 defeat.

24 December 1991

Peter Reid swooped to sign the experienced midfielder
Steve McMahon from Liverpool in a £900,000 move.

24 December 2001

Long-time City groundsman Stan Gibson passed away aged
seventy-six. Gibson had earned plenty of accolades down
the years for the perfect playing surfaces at Maine Road,
and led club secretary Bernard Halford to proclaim that,
'Stan could grow grass on concrete.'

25 December 1902

The first match played between Manchester City and Manchester United in their current guises ended with a 1–1 draw with Billy Meredith scoring for the Blues.

25 December 1933

Frank Swift had a debut to forget as he picked the ball out of the net four times in City's defeat against Derby.

25 December 1957

The 2–1 defeat at Turf Moor against Burnley was the last time that the club played a fixture on Christmas Day.

26 December 1894

City crashed to an 8–0 defeat against Burton Wanderers.

26 December 1913

Future City and England goalkeeper Frank Swift was born in Blackpool.

26 December 1977

After his career was in doubt following the serious injury he suffered in a League Cup tie against Manchester United, Colin Bell returned to the side as a half-time substitute in the Boxing Day clash at home to Newcastle. Describing the moment, manager Tony Book said, 'I sent the team out and followed them down the tunnel. Halfway down I stopped and listened to the roar. It was amazing. I recall the kids hanging over the tunnel and it began with them shouting, "It's him, it's him", and from there it went around the ground.' The applause that greeted Bell's introduction lasted well into the second half and City went on to win the match 4–0.

26 December 1989

A 1–0 win over Norwich signalled the start of Howard Kendall's time in charge at the club.

27 December 1938

City beat Tranmere 5–2 at Maine Road to make it two wins and fourteen goals in consecutive days against the same opponents. It was also a rich time for Jackie Milsom who hit two hat-tricks in the clashes.

27 December 2009

Denying there was a problem with Craig Bellamy – a staunch supporter of Mark Hughes – new manager Roberto Mancini said, 'There is no problem. I spoke with him two days ago. He understood when I told him he wasn't starting. We have two games in three days and I need all the players at 100 per cent.'

28 December 1998

City came from a goal down to beat Stoke 2–1 at Maine Road. It is thought that this win was the catalyst for the side's second-half run that took them into the play-offs as defeat was tasted just twice in twenty-two games following the turn of the year.

28 December 2006

Joey Barton failed in his appeal against his sending-off in the recent game at Bolton and was handed a three-match ban by the FA.

29 December 1917

Billy Meredith put the Blues ahead in their 4–0 wartime
victory away to Blackburn.

30 December 1996

After Phil Neal had held the fort following Steve Coppell's
departure – winning just two of the ten games in charge –
the club appointed Frank Clark as the new manager. Clark
had enjoyed success in charge of Nottingham Forest.
Upon his arrival, Clark set about making immediate
changes behind the scenes – not always popular
decisions – but he would lose just four of his first twenty-
one games in charge.

30 December 2005

With the prospect of European qualification by no
means assured, manager Stuart Pearce admitted that the
possibility of entering the Inter-Toto Cup was something
the club may have to consider.

31 December 2004

Colin Bell was awarded an MBE in the New Year's Honours List for services to the community. Speaking to the *Manchester Evening News*, Bell said, 'I had to read it twice, then ask my wife to do so again. It is something you never expect to happen.'

Acknowledgements & Bibliography

Thanks to my publishers, The History Press, for allowing me the opportunity to bring a spark of an idea to life and to the editors Michelle Tilling and Richard Leatherdale for their assistance and guidance throughout.

To my family for all of their love and support – not to mention an introduction to the club.

Thanks to those in whose company I have spent many hours watching, debating, enjoying, commiserating and exasperating with – all in the name of Manchester City.

And most of all to Faith and Ruby – without their patience and understanding this book would not have been possible.

Books

Clayton, David, *Everything Under The Blue Moon – The Complete Book of Manchester City FC*, Mainstream Publishing, 2002

Clayton, David, *Man City: 50 Classic Matches . . . and Some to Forget!*, The History Press, 2010

Creighton, John, *Manchester City – Moments to Remember*, Sigma Leisure, 1992

James, Gary, *Manchester City The Complete Record*,
    Breedon Books, 2006

James, Gary, *The Big Book of City*, James Ward, 2009

James, Gary, *Manchester City Hall of Fame*, Hamlyn, 2006

Murray, Scott and Walker, Rowan, *Day of The Match*,
    Boxtree, 2008

Penney, Ian, *Manchester City: The Mercer Allison Years*,
    Breedon Books, 2008

Newspapers

The *Guardian*
The *Independent*
Manchester Evening News
The *Mirror*

Websites

bbc.co.uk
bitterandblue.com
fa.com
mcivta.com
mcfcstats.co.uk
mcfc.co.uk
soccerbase.com
statto.com

Other resources

Manchester Central Library archives
The author's own programme collection